Spur-of-the-Moment
CRAFTS

AGES 6-12

NEXGEN®

Building the New Generation of Believers

An Imprint of Cook Communications Ministries
COLORADO SPRINGS, COLORADO • PARIS, ONTARIO
KINGSWAY COMMUNICATIONS, LTD., EASTBOURNE, ENGLAND

NexGen® is an imprint of
Cook Communications Ministries, Colorado Springs, CO 80918
Cook Communications, Paris, Ontario
Kingsway Communications, Eastbourne, England

SPUR-OF-THE-MOMENT CRAFTS
©1996, 2004 Cook Communications Ministries

First Printing, 1996
First NexGen Printing, 2004
Printed in United States of America
1 2 3 4 5 6 7 8 9 10 Printing/Year 08 07 06 05 04

Editorial Manager: Doug Schmidt
Product Developer: Karen Pickering
Designed by: Barnstorm Visual Communications
Art Spots/Craft Illustrations: Kurt Holdorf, Holdorf Design

ISBN: 07814-4121-8

Spur-of-the-Moment CRAFTS

Contents

INTRODUCTION

The lesson has been taught. The lesson activities are finished. The class is over . . . but there are several minutes left in the hour . . . or church has run longer than expected. Perhaps a lesson has gone faster than planned; maybe you sense the need for another activity to reinforce a biblical truth; perhaps the children are restless, or students arrive in the classroom several minutes early.

If you are a volunteer in the children's department of any church, you've faced those times when you need an extra activity to help keep children interested and actively involved.

It is for these situations that this book is written. *Spur-of-the-Moment Crafts* gives you the tools you need to keep children in grades 1-6 interested. You do not have to round up extra materials, run to the copier, or sit and trace patterns. These crafts are designed to give you spur-of-the-moment flexibility and creativity without extra work. Crafts that take longer than a few minutes can be continued the following week. Keep in mind that almost all crafts require more than the primary ingredient. So while a craft might be listed under Construction Paper Crafts, you will probably also need other supplies such as scissors, crayons or markers, paper plates, etc.

Do you have a crafts cupboard in your classroom or close by? Keep these 25 items in it or your classroom, and you will be able to provide an instant craft for your students.

And if your church cannot provide all of these items, encourage your parents to get involved and contribute one item from each family. Or, organize a cookie bake and use the money from that to purchase them. Put a notice in the church bulletin asking for these specific supplies. Ask your youth group to donate, help organize the cupboard, and be your classroom craft helpers. Be creative. Your children and your church will benefit.

25 Craft Items to Keep on Hand

Bibles—a must for any classroom of children who need to know that they are learning what God says, not just the teacher.

Construction paper—in multiple colors.

Craft Sticks—look like popsicle sticks and often come in packages of 100.

Crayons—4-6 boxes of 24 or more colors will let all children have access at the same time. Keep more on hand if possible or have one 12-crayon package for each child.

Chenille Stems—come in packages of various colors; have several packages available.

Glitter—keep various colors ready for use.

Glue—at least 1 bottle for every 3 students.

Hole punch—at least one, preferably three will make this part of an activity go more smoothly.

Magazines/Catalogs—have parents contribute; nature magazines and family magazines are especially good.

Markers—be sure they are washable. These come in packages like crayons; same recommendation.

Newsprint rolls—could also use the freezer wrap paper available in grocery stores.

Paper bags—plain brown, white, colored; parents may be willing to send one package with their child once a quarter.

Paper fasteners—brads come in packages of 100; keep 2-3 packages handy.

Paper plates—most discount stores sell these in packages of 100. Keep at least one full package, two if you have room.

Plain white paper—usually comes in reams (500 sheets), can be copier paper or computer paper.

Rulers—keep several 12-inch rulers, 2 to 3 18-inch rulers, and a yardstick handy.

Scissors—at least 1 pair for every 2 students but enough for each child to have his/her own is recommended.

Straws—keep 2-3 large packages of at least 100 each in your cupboard.

Foam cups—most discount stores sell these in packages of 100. Keep at least one full package, two if you have room.

Tape—keep cellophane and masking tape handy, at least 1 roll (on a dispenser) for every 3-4 students. The 3/4" wide tape is better than the 1/2" wide tape. One inch wide is also good.

Stapler/staples—keep at least 3-4 in your classroom, fully loaded. Perhaps an early-arrival student could be responsible for checking the staplers and being sure they are filled each week.

Yarn/string—keep at least one full roll of string and yarn in a variety of colors.

Paint shirts/smocks—keep shirts or smocks handy for projects that can get messy.

Spur~of~the~Moment HINTS— General

All measurements given with these crafts are guidelines. Shapes and sizes do not have to be exact. It will take more time than necessary if teacher and students are concerned with making exact squares, strips, and circles. Here are a few hints to help keep these crafts simple and quick:

Easy squares—4-inch squares are used in many of the crafts. Fold a sheet of construction paper in half vertically, then in thirds. Cut or tear on each fold line. Copier or computer paper will work about the same, with slightly smaller squares.

Easy circle—Trace the top or bottom of a foam cup.

Easy large circles—Fold any size paper in fourths (half and then half again), then cut off the corners. Fold out into a circle.

Easy straight edge—If you don't have enough rulers to go around, try using a flattened straw, a craft stick, or a piece of paper folded in half.

Easy 1-inch strips—Most rulers are about an inch wide. Trace the ruler and cut.

Easy 1-inch squares—Use the ruler again. Trace lines one direction, then the other.

Spur~of~the~Moment HINTS— Paints

Paints add excitement to any craft project. Most of the projects in this book that call for coloring can be changed to a painting craft.

Keep any type of washable paints in your craft closet. Acrylics and tempera are available in small bottles that are easy to store. Watercolors will also work well with most of the crafts.

If you don't have an abundance of brushes, use cotton swabs or cotton balls. Or, try one of these alternatives:

• Drop some paint onto paper and then blow on paint through a straw to make a design.

• Drop some paint onto a surface and smash the dots of paint with a piece of paper bag.

• Form a stamp with chenille stem and stamp designs onto paper or surface.

• Smear paint onto surface with the end of a craft stick.

• Dip the bottom of a foam cup into paint and stamp the circle design onto paper.

• Dip yarn into paint, then lay yarn out carefully onto surface. Press down to stamp design onto surface. Then, carefully remove yarn.

• Dip cotton ball into paint. Blot it onto the paper or surface. Press down hard in some spots and press lightly in others to make a variety of designs.

Keep plenty of paper towels in your closet. Fill foam cups with water to clean brushes and other paint items. Be sure to use paint shirts or smocks to protect children's clothing.

Spur~of~the~Moment HINTS— Alternatives to Coloring

Some children, especially upper elementary aged students, simply do not enjoy coloring. In order to have a craft that is enjoyable to all students, try some of these alternatives to coloring with crayons.

Use any of the painting techniques above. Also,

have a variety of other items to use with paints.

• *Toothbrushes.* Students can paint with a toothbrush for a different texture than with paintbrushes.

• Alternative: Spatter paint by filling the toothbrush bristles with paint, then rubbing the bristles gently with the long edge of a craft stick. (Hold toothbrush about 6 inches or less above the paper and rub the stick AWAY from body to avoid spattering on clothing. Have children wear paint shirts.)

• *Sponges.* Dampen sponge pieces (various sizes) with water. Dip into paint, then spread on paper as with a brush.

• Alternative: Cut sponges into pieces of various sizes (1-3 inches). Dip into paint and press onto paper. Overlap colors by waiting until first color is dry, then use a different color to overlap the paint spots. (Have children wear paint shirts.)

• *Texture paints.* Provide various items to dip into paint and press onto paper. Ideas: Nylon dish scrubber. Stiff-bristled brush (household scrub brushes). Cotton balls. Tennis ball. Comb. Fork. (Have children wear paint shirts.)

Spur-of-the-Moment HINTS— Crayon Variations

• Create a *stained glass* look. Use this technique only on plain paper. After coloring the picture with crayons, rub baby oil lightly all over the page with a cotton ball.

• Create *secret colors* by coloring different colors of stripes across the coloring area, pressing heavily with crayon. Then, cover entire area very darkly with black crayon. Next, use a fairly sharp pointed item, such as pencil with broken lead, pen with tip retracted, or end of a craft stick to scratch a picture through the black crayon surface.

• Create a *sandpaper texture* by slipping a piece of sandpaper under coloring area and using a crayon to color. Several different textures of sandpaper can be used to make a variety of textures.

• Create a *sandpaper picture* by coloring ON a piece of sandpaper. Then, glue the sandpaper to craft surface.

• Create *crayon shavings* by removing paper from several colors of crayons. Use an opened scissors to shave bits and curls from the side of crayons. Spread glue onto picture and sprinkle the crayon shavings over glue.

• Create *mosaics* by filling in any coloring area with glue and dropping small bits of construction paper that has been cut into a variety of shapes onto glue.

• Alternatives: Use brightly colored magazine pages in place of construction paper. Or, color bits of a foam cup and glue the colored bits to picture.

• Create *crumples* by crumpling small bits of any type paper and gluing to coloring area.

• Create *paper curls* by cutting 1/2 x 1-inch strips of any brightly colored paper. Curl strips around a pencil, then glue to coloring area.

• Create *chenille curls* by cutting 2-inch lengths of chenille stems. Roll lengths into a circle, then glue flat onto picture.

• Create *yarn fill-ins* by cutting up small bits of yarn. Spread glue onto coloring area and sprinkle yarn bits into the glue. Press down slightly.

• Alternatives: Bring any of these items from home and use for fill-ins: Macaroni/pasta, cereal, marshmallows, rice, beans/peas, wood shavings bars of colored soaps to shave, cotton balls, styrofoam packing bits.

• Create *sparkle and shine* by using various colors of glitter in place of or in addition to coloring.

CONSTRUCTION PAPER CRAFTS

1

BASKET IDEAS

THINGS YOU'LL NEED...

- ☐ 8.5" x 11" pieces of construction paper – multiple colors
- ☐ Ruler
- ☐ Scissors
- ☐ Pencils
- ☐ Crayons or colored markers
- ☐ Glue or tape
- ☐ Glitter
- ☐ Paper plates

General instructions for basket

Cut bottom of basket by folding a piece of 8.5 x 11 inch construction paper in half horizontally. Draw half a hexagon on the fold (a 2-inch line up from fold at about 30 degrees, a 2-inch line straight across, and another 2-inch line back down toward the fold). Cut out the half hexagon, then unfold basket bottom. It will have six edges.

Sides are made from six identical shapes, as in the ideas below. Bottom edge of shapes will be 2-3 inches to fit the 2-inch sections of the hexagon. (Shapes can overlap each other slightly.) Shapes can be wider at middle and top or the same width at the bottom.

Tape or glue bottom edge of each piece to basket bottom. Then fold up and tape or glue the side of each piece to the side of the next piece.

For an optional handle, cut a strip of paper 10 inches long and 1-2 inches wide. Tape or glue handle inside the top edge of two sections directly across from each other.

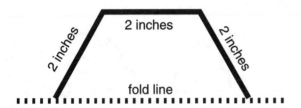

2 inches

2 inches · 2 inches

fold line

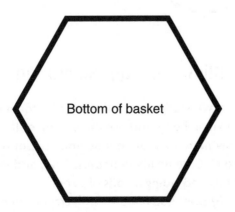

Bottom of basket

SEASONAL BASKETS

1. Valentine or Love Theme-Hearts

Cut out six hearts of pink or red, or two each of pink, red, and white. Alternate colors when putting basket together. To cut hearts, fold construction paper in half vertically, then into thirds horizontally. This forms six sections. Cut the six sections apart, then draw and cut a heart from each section. Tape the bottom edge of each heart to one 2-inch section of the hexagon. Then fold up the hearts and tape or glue each side together.

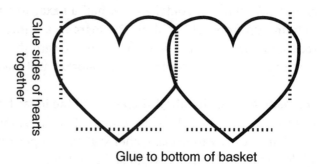

Glue sides of hearts together

Glue to bottom of basket

2. Winter Theme-Snowflakes

Cut out six 3-inch circles. Fold each circle into fourths, and cut out triangular holes on each fold. Unfold and tape snowflakes to bottom of basket, overlapping edges slightly. Then tape or glue sides of snowflakes together for basket.

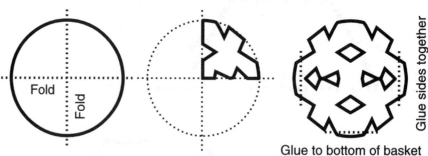

Fold

Fold

Glue sides together

Glue to bottom of basket

3. Winter Theme-Snowmen

Have students use the top of a foam cup as the pattern for the snowman body, and use the bottom of the cup as the pattern for the snowman head. Six heads and six bodies should be cut for each basket. Glue heads to bodies. Then add eyes, noses, and mouths by cutting and gluing on bits of paper.

Option: Add features with crayons or colored markers.

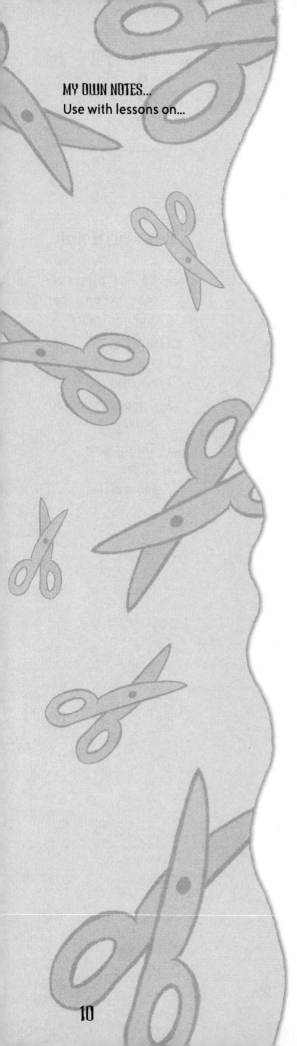

Cut a black 1-inch square for each snowman; glue to top of head for hat. Tape or glue bottom of each snowman to basket bottom; then tape or glue together at middle of each snowmen to form the basket.

4. Spring Theme-Bird Nests

Cut three circles, slightly larger than the top of a foam cup. Cut each circle in half. Draw lines with a marker or crayon to look like a nest. Cut small oblongs or circles from blue paper to make baby bird heads. Draw eyes and a beak on each. Cut out the beak. Glue one or two baby bird heads on top of each nest. Put basket together as in others above.

Can also be used with creation lesson, Noah, and with Matthew 10:29-31—God's care of sparrows and His children.

5. Easter Theme-Crosses

Cut out strips of paper 2 inches wide and 4 to 6 inches long. Cut out crossbars which are 3 to 4 inches long and 1 inch wide. Tape or glue crosses together at the crossbar. Then tape or glue the bottom of the crosses to the bottom of the basket. Use a single long strip of paper at the top and glue or tape top of crosses to it.

6. Summer Theme-Flags

Cut out six 2-inch squares of white. Draw red stripes and a blue square in the upper left-hand corner. (Students may cut red stripes and glue them on instead of coloring.) Bottom of basket can be red, white, or blue.

Option: Flags can be adapted for any country. e.g. Canada—Use white squares for the back-ground. Color a red stripe at the left and right side of the flag and freehand draw a red maple leaf in the center. Construct basket as above.

7. Thanksgiving Theme-Home

Cut out six 2-inch wide house shapes. They can be as tall as the students like. Students may add doors and windows with markers or of construction paper. Write on at least one of the houses—*I thank God for my home.* Other houses could bear statements of other things for which students are thankful. Construct basket as above.

8. Serving-Hands

Have students trace their handprints on paper and cut out at least six of them. Write out a verse such as Joshua 24:15; Psalm 90:17, or Ecclesiastes 9:10a on the handprints. Tape palm ends to basket bottom with fingers pointing upward.

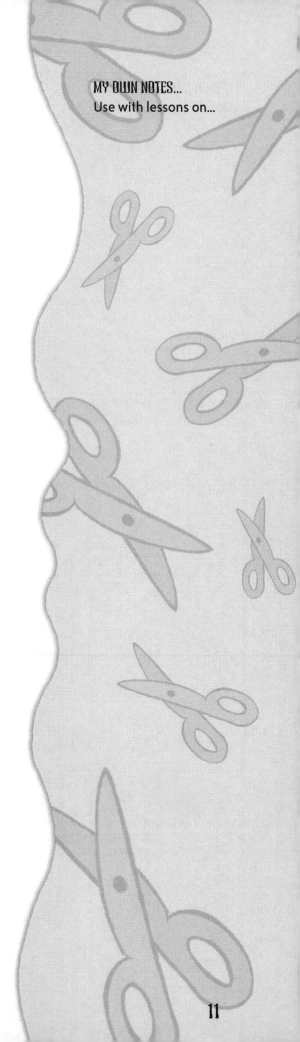

9. Worship-Church

Make houses as above, then cut out a steeple and glue it to the top of each.

Write out a verse such as Psalm 26:8, 92:13, 122:1 or Proverbs 9:1, 12:7b, or Acts 5:42. Glue edges of churches together to form sides and glue bottom of churches to bottom of basket sides.

Glue to bottom of basket

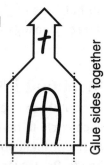

Glue sides together

WOVEN BASKETS

10. Colorful Paper Weaving

On 8-1/2" x 11" construction paper, cut 3-inch long slits at each corner, angled toward center of paper. Fold up sides and glue or tape together as illustrated. On the two long sides of basket, cut four slits from the bottom, almost to the top. One slit should be at each corner and the other two about 1-1/2 to 2 inches from each corner. Then, cut out two or three 1/2-inch wide strips of paper, 7 inches long—each a different color. Weave the strips in and out through the slits and tape at the ends. Do the same on the other side of basket. Add a handle made from a 2" x 10" strip. Use holiday colors, seasonal colors, or just your favorites.

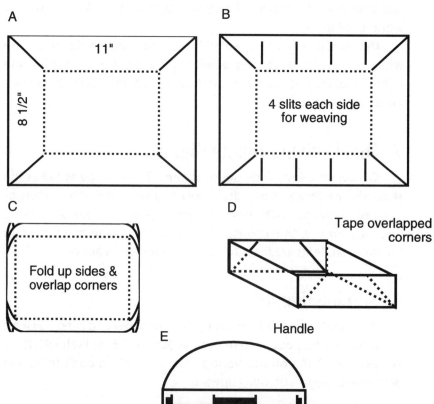

A

11"

8 1/2"

B

4 slits each side for weaving

C

Fold up sides & overlap corners

D

Tape overlapped corners

Handle

E

Basket can be used to reinforce lesson on Feeding the 5,000 (write Matt. 14:13-21 on the handle) or Moses in the Bulrushes (write Exod. 2:1-3 or Heb. 11:23-29 on the handle). Basket can also be used on a desk or dresser to keep odds and ends in.

11. Joseph's Coat—Yarn Weave

As above, but weave multi-colored lengths of yarn through the slits on the basket. Cut lengths of yarn and weave bunches of five at a time. Tape the lengths of yarn together at both ends. Write on the basket handle, *My Father Loves Me*.

Basket can be used to reinforce story of Joseph's coat of many colors. Can also help children think about how much Jacob loved Joseph and use it to remind them that God loved Joseph even more, and did wonderful things in Joseph's life. God also loves us and will do wonderful things in our lives.

12. Yarn Wrap

Cut a five-sided basket bottom or a round one. Cut five pieces of paper 2 inches wide by 3 inches long. Tape or glue the 2-inch ends of the pieces to the bottom of the basket. Then cut one-yard lengths of bright colors of yarn. Tape the end of a length of yarn to one of the side pieces and begin to weave loosely over and under the five pieces. The sides will begin to stand upright as the yarn is woven over and under the pieces of paper. Students may use as many yarn lengths as desired to finish the basket. Tie each new length to the end of the previous one and continue to weave.

Make a handle from a strip of paper about 2" x 8". Write on the handle, *God's Love Gives Me Joy*.

Basket can be used to reinforce the truth of how God's love weaves joy and strength into our lives.

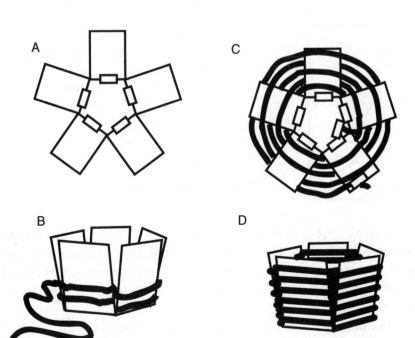

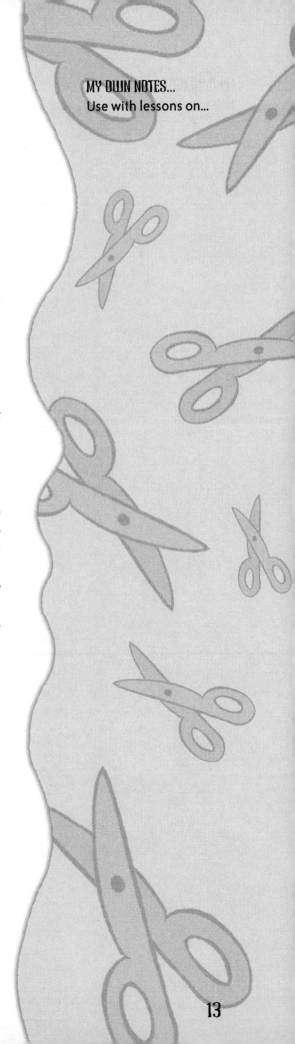

BOOKMARKS

13. Heart Bookmark

Fold a piece of red or pink construction paper in half vertically. On the fold, cut a half heart, about 2" high and 1" to 2" wide. Use this shape to trace and cut three more hearts. Glue hearts together top to bottom, then glue strip of hearts onto a 1" wide by 10" long piece of construction paper.

Option: Cut one 10" length of yarn. Glue one heart shape at the top end of the yarn and glue another heart one-half of the way down the first heart so they overlap. Do the same thing with the other two hearts at the bottom end of the yarn. Finished bookmark will have a heart at each end of the yarn length.

Use to reinforce lessons on our love for each other or God's love for us.

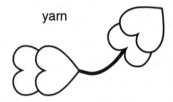

yarn

14. Christmas Tree Bookmark

From green paper, cut one Christmas tree shape (a triangle; add jagged edges) about 3" high and 2" to 3" wide. Use this shape to trace and cut out 3 more of increasing sizes. Cut a 10" length of green or white yarn and glue the tree bookmark together as in the Heart Bookmark.

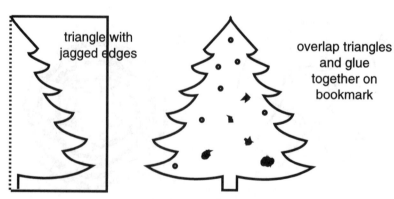

triangle with jagged edges

overlap triangles and glue together on bookmark

Option: Use a hole punch to make open circles. Glue colored paper to the back of the tree to add bright colors. Or, use the hole punch to make brightly colored circles from other pieces of construction paper and glue those onto the original green Christmas tree.

Option: Use star or dot stickers to decorate the trees.

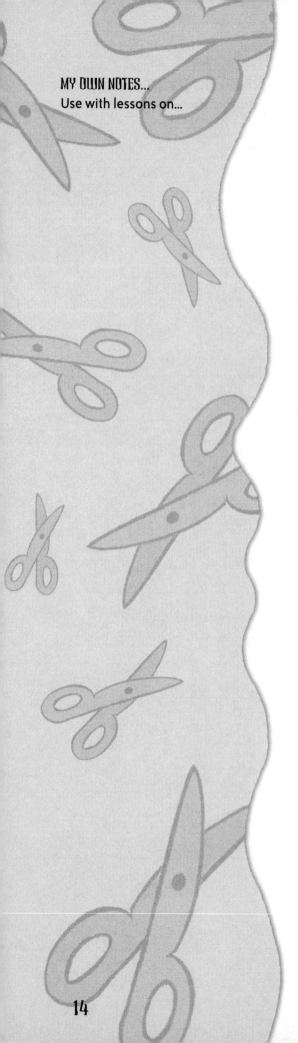

15. Cross Bookmark

Cut one cross about 2" long with a crossbar of 1" to 1-1/2". Make as above with either a 10" piece of construction paper or brown yarn.

16. Shamrock Bookmark

Cut out four shamrock shapes. (It's easier to cut on fold of paper.) Cut one 10" length of green or white yarn. Glue shamrocks together, placing about 1/2" of the yarn in between them. Do the same at the other end of the length of yarn.

shamrock
shape

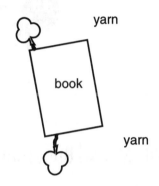

yarn

book

yarn

17. Caterpillar Bookmark

Cut a 1" x 6" piece of construction paper. Take the bottom of a foam cup (or use a quarter) and trace a series of rounded halves. Cut the rounded edges. Draw eyes and a mouth on the first one. Add yarn or chenille stems for antennae.

18. Turtle Bookmark

Cut out a green circle to make the turtle's shell. Glue a few small yellow bits of paper to the turtle's shell. Cut the head and four legs from yellow or brown paper and glue to the shell. Draw eyes and mouth on the head. Glue turtle to a craft stick or the small end of a 1" wide, 7" long piece of construction paper or yarn.

yarn

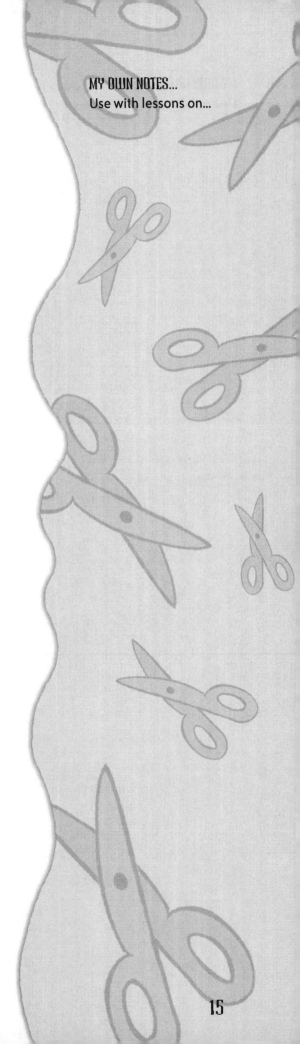

19. Ladybug Bookmark

Cut out a red circle and fold in the middle. Add black circles made with hole punch from black paper or small black sticker-dots. Cut out a small half circle from black paper and glue to edge of the red circle. Cut six 1" long pieces of black yarn and glue three to each side of the circle for legs. Glue on a piece of black yarn or small, thin pieces of black paper for feelers. Glue on yarn of any color or glue ladybug to small end of a 1" wide, 6" long piece of paper.

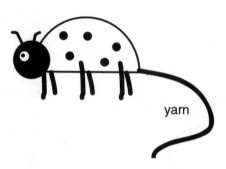

yarn

20. Mouse Bookmark

Cut out a gray circle and fold it in half to make the mouse's body. Cut a six-inch piece of pink yarn for a tail. Unfold the gray circle and place about one inch of the pink yarn on the fold line. Spread glue on the inside of the circle and refold, making sure that the yarn is secured inside the fold.

On the outside of the shape, add a face at the opposite end from yarn tail. Draw an eye on each side of the mouse.

Cut two ovals for ears. Pinch one end of each to make a partial fold. Glue the pinched ends of the ears on the mouse, just above the eyes. (Ears will point upward.) Punch a pink circle with the hole punch. Fold in half. Glue circle on front edge of fold line for nose with the fold over the fold of the mouse's body. Or cut a tiny pink nose from paper or draw on one with a marker. Add a few glued-on strands of black, white, or gray yarn for whiskers.

pink yarn

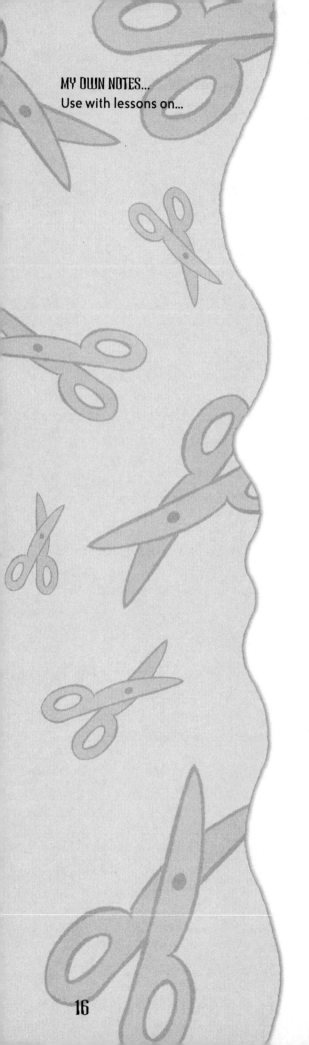

21. Smiling Sun Bookmark

Cut a circle from bright yellow paper. Draw eyes and big smile. Glue circle to a craft stick or to the small end of a 1" x 6" piece of construction paper. Children may want to write, "Jesus is my Sonshine" on this bookmark.

DOORKNOB HANGERS

Basic directions:

Fold and cut a sheet of 8 1/2" x 11" construction paper in half vertically (long side to long side) to make a 4 1/4" x 11" inch piece. About 2" from the top, cut out a circle, about 2" wide, as illustrated. Then, cut a slit in four spots on the circle. Slits should be about 1" long. These slits will allow the hanger to fit over a doorknob without tearing the paper.

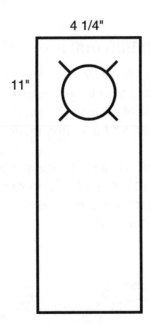

22. Glitter Hanger

Students can write their name, Jesus, or another thematic word on front of hanger. Then, have them outline the letters in glue, and sprinkle glitter onto the glue.

Option: Outline entire doorknob hanger and/or write name in star or dot stickers.

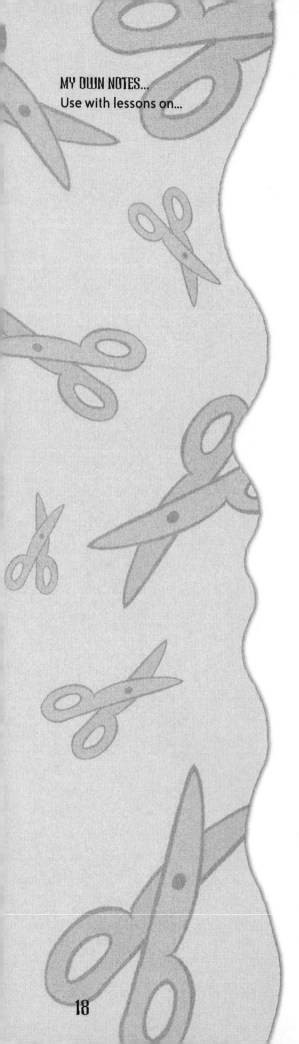

23. Heart Hanger

Place a piece of red paper and a piece of black paper together. Cut hearts from both pieces of paper at the same time. Hearts can be cut by folding any sized piece of paper in half and cutting the heart shape from the fold side.

On red hearts write: "For God so loved the world." Glue the black hearts on first, then glue the red hearts on top of them but a little to one side of the black heart to make a shadow look.

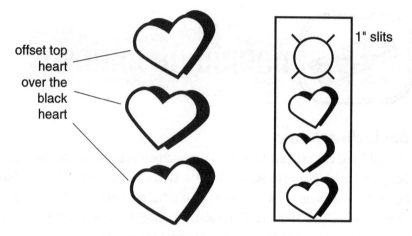

offset top heart over the black heart

1" slits

Glue hearts onto the basic doorknob hanger.

24. Question and Answer Hanger

Students make four circles from a bright color and four circles from black. Write: "Jesus is the answer" on the four bright circles. Then layer the black circles behind the colored ones for a shadow look (as above). With marker, add question marks in several spots on the doorknob hanger.

Or, students can cut out a question mark from the vertical length of an 8-1/2" x 11" sheet of colored paper and from a piece of black paper. Layer as described. Write: "Jesus is the answer" and hang with the crook of the question mark.

FLAGS

25. American Flag

Turn a whole sheet of white paper horizontal. Cut four red stripes, 11" long, 1" wide. Glue the stripes onto the white paper, leaving approximately 1/2" between each strip of red paper. Add a blue corner and star stickers can be used if desired. Otherwise, use small pieces of white paper for the stars.

Glue two 11" long and 1" wide strips of brown paper together end to end as the flagpole. Glue to left side of flag. On the brown strips write: "Free to Love and Worship God."

Option: Flags can be adapted for any country. e.g. Canada—Use white sheet of paper. Cut two 3" x 8-1/2" strips of red. Glue one strip to each side of paper. Draw a red maple leaf in the center, trace a real leaf, or glue the real leaf in the middle. Add flagpole as above.

26. Christian Flag

Glue a 2" x 3" blue rectangle in the upper left corner of a sheet of white paper. Add a red cross in the middle of the blue field. Students may write a verse or the entire Pledge to the Christian Flag.

I pledge allegiance to the Christian flag and to the Savior for whose kingdom it stands. One Savior, crucified, risen, and coming again with life and liberty for all who believe.

27. Family or Classroom Flag

Give students paper and markers and let them create their own flags. Encourage them to make them distinctive to their own families, special activities they enjoy together, etc.

Use with a lesson about being part of God's family, or an Old Testament lesson to reinforce the nation of Israel and how it was established.

Option: You may want to provide a modern Israeli flag as inspiration.

FOLDED PAPER

28. Folded Paper Heart

Fold a sheet of white paper in half. Cut a large heart out of it. Then cut lots of red squares, fold corners as in Folded Paper Texture Wreath craft (#29). Cover your heart with squares. Add a loop of yarn for hanging.

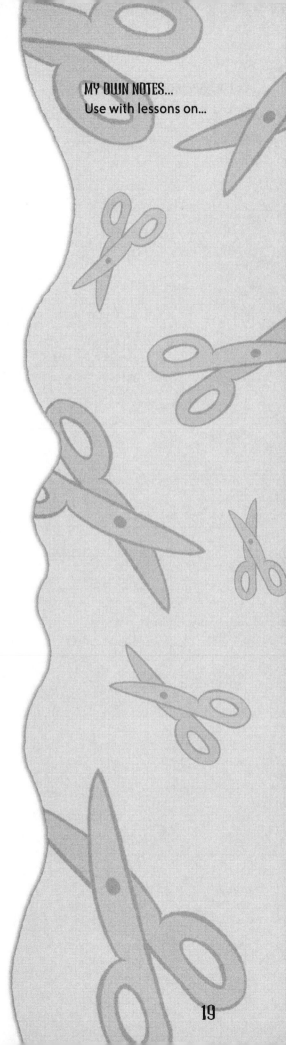

29. Folded Paper Texture Wreath

Cut the middle from a paper plate. Cut lots of paper squares about 2" x 2" or larger. Use one color or several. (For example: Orange, brown, and yellow for fall. Red, green, and white for Christmas. Red or pink for Valentine's day. Pastels for spring.)

To curl the corners of the squares, lay a pencil or craft stick across the square, diagonally. Roll each side of the square over the pencil or stick.

Glue flat bottom of squares as close together as possible onto plate rim. Add yarn loop for hanging.

Option: Glue a paper bow or a cutout such as candle, big blue star, cross, or big red heart to the bottom inside edge of wreath center. Bow should drape over the bottom portion of wreath.

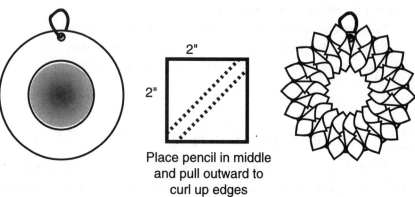

Place pencil in middle and pull outward to curl up edges

FOLDED SQUARES

30. Folded Paper Angel

Cut two 4" squares of white paper and a pink 2" circle. (Trace the bottom of a foam cup onto paper and cut out.)

Fold one square in half diagonally. Fold the other over from each corner to make an upside-down V as shown.

Glue halved square onto other one as shown. Add circle for angel's head. Use with any lessons that include angels.

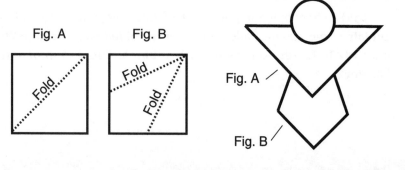

Fig. A   Fig. B

Fold

Fold

Fold

Fig. A

Fig. B

31. Three-Tiered Tree

Cut three 4" squares from green paper. Fold one square in half diagonally for the bottom tier.

Fold another square in half diagonally, then in half diagonally again. This is the second tier.

For the top tier, fold a square in half diagonally three times. Stagger tiers on top of each other and staple in place. Decorations can be made by using a hole punch to make round holes from several colors of paper. Add lines of glitter to look like garlands. Top the tree with some gold glitter. A trunk can be cut from brown paper and glued to the bottom of tree, if desired.

Option: Make small circles; draw faces on them to represent family members. Place them in each tier of the tree as it is glued.

32. Verse Tree

Make a Three-Tiered Tree as above, but write verses on each tier before assembling. Possible verses: Proverbs 11:30; Matthew 7:17; John 1:50b; Revelation 2:7. Add glitter to the edges of tree.

33. Folded Paper Star

Cut five 4" squares from yellow paper (or dark blue). (Cut smaller squares for a smaller star.) Fold all five squares in half diagonally. Position on flat surface. Overlap corners of long, folded edges slightly, with the mid-points facing in, as shown.

Glue or tape together at points. Mount on dark blue construction paper (or yellow).

Use with any lesson emphasizing a star such as the Christmas lesson (Matt. 2:2, 10) or with such verses/studies as: Revelation 2:28; 2 Peter 1:19; Revelation 1:16; Genesis 1:16. Make the star brighter by adding gold glitter. Staple on a yarn loop to hang the star.

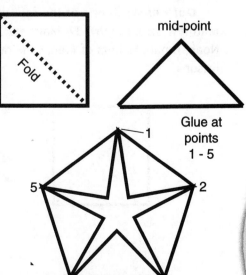

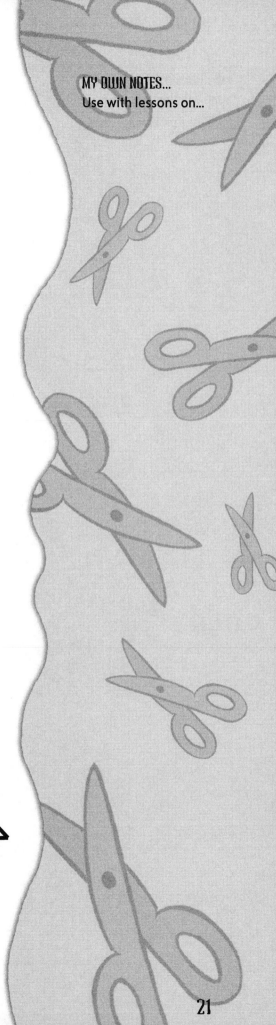

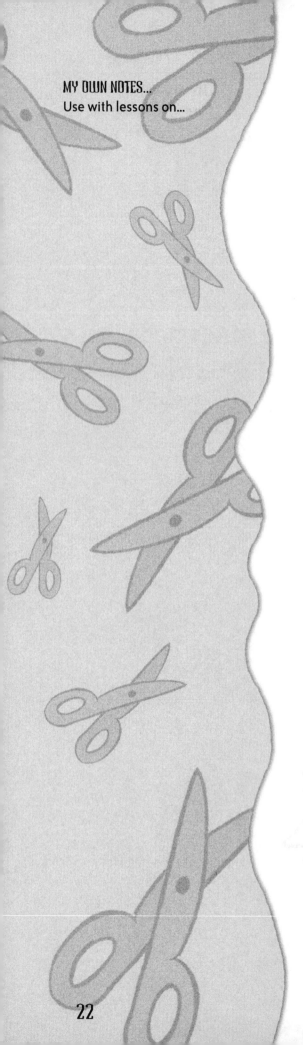

34. Butterfly Mobile

Cut pairs of brightly colored 4" squares. For each butterfly, fold two matching squares in half diagonally and glue, staple, or fasten together with brads at one end.

Tape or staple a length of yarn to each butterfly.

To make the mobile, punch holes in the edge of a paper plate and hang at least five butterflies from the plate. Also punch two holes in the middle of plate and attach yarn through both holes to make loop for hanging.

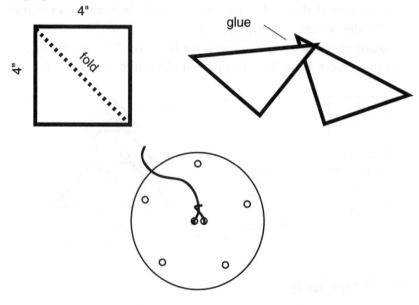

35. Fish Mobile

Cut pairs of brightly colored 4" squares of paper as above. Fold two pieces in half and slip together as shown.

Glue (or staple) and add yarn to hang.

To make the mobile, punch holes in the edge of a paper plate and hang at least five fish from the plate. Also, punch two holes in the middle of plate and attach yarn through both holes to make loop for hanging.

Option: Write one of the following verses on the edge of plate: Matthew 4:19; Jonah 1:17; Matthew 17:27. Can be used with Creation, Noah, Jonah, Fishers of Men, or Miracle of Tax Money in Fish's Mouth lessons.

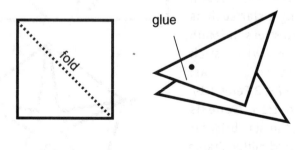

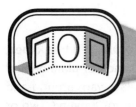

FRAMES

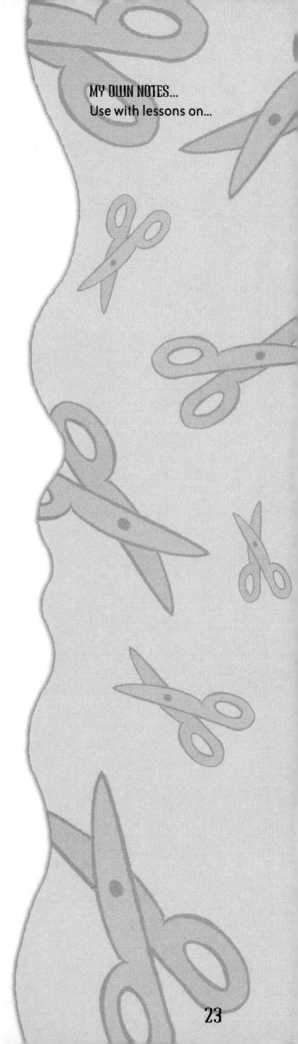

36. Standing Tri-Fold Frame

Fold one piece of paper in half horizontally (top to bottom, short side to short side).

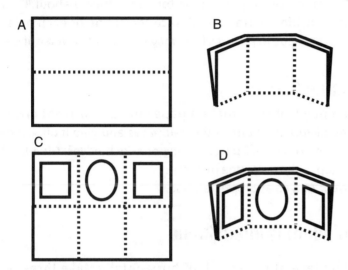

Then fold that into thirds to make a standing frame. Unfold and cut one hole in top half of each section of frame. Can make two rectangles and a circle as shown. Re-fold the paper and put a staple at each fold. Pictures can be slipped in through the top of the frame and taped in place with a small piece of tape inside the frame attached to the back of the picture.

Option: Decorate frames with stickers, markers, glitter, etc.

37. Standing Single Frame

Fold paper in half as above. Then, fold into standing frame as shown.

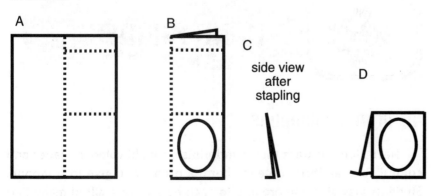

Cut a hole for the picture, then staple and stand. Picture will be slipped into frame from the open side.

Option: Students may wish to write a verse on the frame.

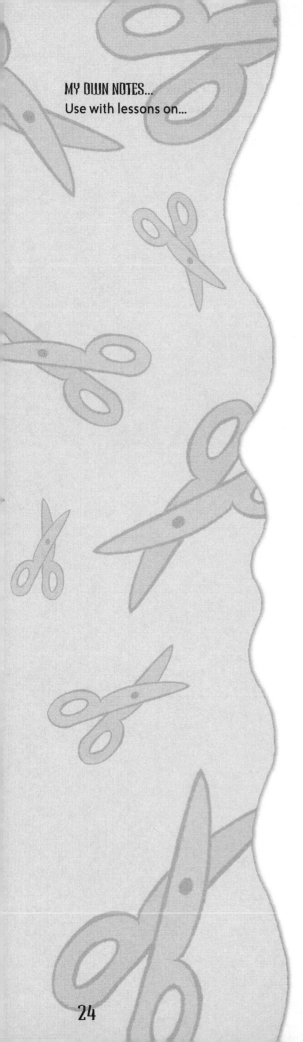

38. Paper Plate Frames

Cut out a shape in the middle of one plate. It could be a tree, a bell, an oblong, etc. Tape a picture inside the shape. Fit another plate behind the picture. Then, staple, glue, or punch holes to lace yarn around and through the edges of both plates. Add a yarn loop for hanging. Two or three wallet-sized photos will fit in one plate, if you choose.

Option: If frames won't be used as a gift, or you don't want students to have to go home and find a picture of themselves, use this alternative. Cut out three pieces of paper (one for single frame) about 4" square. Slip paper inside the frame and trace the shape of each hole. Take papers out and glue in pictures from magazines. Add a verse, if desired.

39. Framed Scene

Cut a piece of construction paper in half horizontally. Find a magazine picture to fit one of the half pages and glue it on. Cut out the middle of the other half page, leaving one-inch edges. Glue the frame piece on top of the magazine picture.

Option: Add an appropriate verse.

40. Window Framed Scene

Cut a piece of paper in half horizontally. Make three or four "window" flaps by cutting the sides and bottom but not the top in one of the half pages. Place the piece of paper with the window flaps over the other rectangle and lightly trace the windows in pencil. Then cut out a small magazine picture for each window and glue it onto the traced areas. Glue the window flap rectangle over the one with pictures. Children can lift the flaps to see the pictures underneath.

Option: On each window, write a prayer thought for the picture. Ideas: "You make awesome sunsets, Lord." "Help me to keep your world beautiful."

HAND SHAPES

41. Promise Coupons

Have students trace their handprints on multi-colors of paper and cut out several. Write on each hand a promise to give to someone. Students may give one promise to each person, or a gift of many tied together with yarn. Promises might include: "Help prepare a meal." "Rake the yard or shovel snow." "Pray for someone specific everyday." "Write a letter for an elderly person."

Reinforces biblical themes of helping, honoring parents, serving.

42. Talents Wreath

Students trace their handprints and cut out several. Write a talent on each hand. (Draw, play instrument, help around the house, be friendly to strangers, pray for others, etc.) Then glue handprints in a circle as shown.

To make wreath stronger, the hands can be glued around the edge of a paper plate. Cut out center of plate and use the rim.

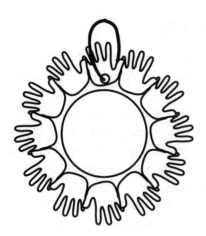

43. Praying Hands Cards

Fold a piece of paper in half vertically (long side to long side). Have students trace their handprints, keeping the little finger side on the fold. Cut out the handprints but do not cut the folded edge.

Students write: "I'm praying for you" on the inside of the card and sign their name.

Option: Students may select a picture from a magazine to glue inside and write a brief note of encouragement.

44. Helper Wall Hanging

Draw four handprints on paper and cut out. Glue or tape hands together as shown.

Write these words in the middle: "Jesus is my Helper." Or, students may write: "I can help Mom and Dad." Attach a yarn loop for hanging.

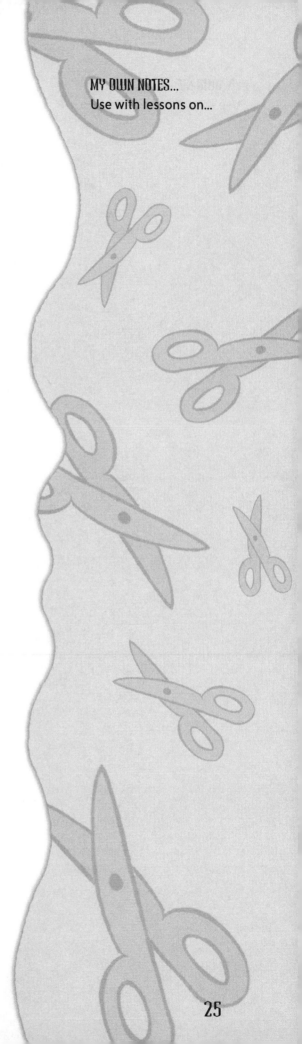

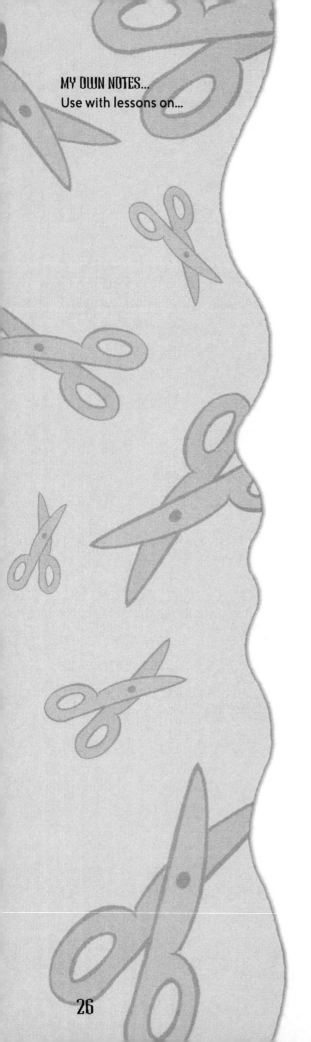

45. Snowflakes

Cut four handprints from white paper. Cut triangle, square, and diamond shapes from center of each hand. Attach the hands together as in the Helper Wall Hanging. Snowflakes can be hung from ceiling or in a window.

46. Rainbow Mobile

Cut five or more handprints from white paper. Color each finger a different color, extending the color into palm of hand. Color both sides of each hand.

To make mobile: Cut a plate in half and draw lines for the seven rainbow colors. Color. (Rainbow colors from bottom to top are: red, orange, yellow, green, blue, indigo, violet.) Punch two holes at top edge for yarn loop. Then, along bottom, punch a hole for each handprint rainbow to hang.

Option: Write one of the following verses on the plate before coloring: Genesis 9:13a; Hebrews 6:12b; 2 Peter 1:4a; 1 John 2:25.

47. Friendship Necklace

Students cut out a handprint for each student in the class and write their name on each one. Classmates exchange handprints with each other. Then, punch a hole in each handprint and string onto a piece of yarn long enough to go loosely around the neck.

Option: Can also be done as a Family Necklace. Have students write names of parents, brothers, sisters, grandparents, cousins, aunts, uncles, etc.

48. Key to Heaven

Have students place hands with fingertips together. Another student traces this praying hand outline. Cut out one praying hands print. If a model is available, trace and/or draw a key. Cut it out. Attach it to the praying hands cut-out with a paper fastener or glue.

Can be used with lessons on prayer. Write on each hand: "Prayer is the key to Heaven."

HEART SHAPES

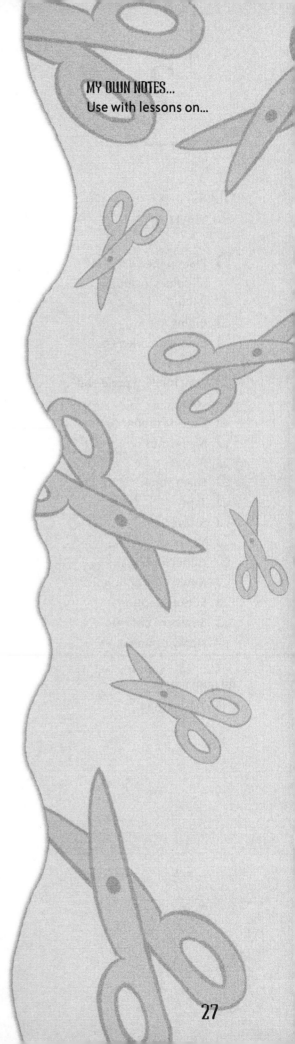

49. People I Love Wall Hanging

Cut several hearts of any size from red or pink paper. Write names of people God has given them to love: family members, friends, teachers, pastor, etc.

Then, glue the hearts together by overlapping the tops to bottoms in a straight line. Add yarn loop to top heart.

Options: Write on hearts: "I am thankful for . . . "; "I love Jesus because . . . "; or, "Ways I can show my love for Jesus . . . ".

50. Friendship Heart Necklace

Fold a full-sized piece of paper vertically (long side to long side). Cut a large heart from it. Then, draw lines and cut heart into at least four pieces as shown.

Punch a hole in each piece and add a length of yarn to fit around neck loosely. Each student gives all but one piece to friends. They keep one piece to wear themselves.

Option: Write Philippians 1:3 on each piece. (Have them look up this verse and read it before completing craft.)

hole for yarn

51. Love Squad Badges

Cut a heart of any size and color. In center of heart, write: "God's Love Squad." Decorate with glitter, markers, stickers, etc.

Tape or pin heart on clothing as a badge as a reminder that God wants us to love others.

2

THINGS
YOU'LL NEED...

- ❑ Plain paper, 8.5" x 11", all colors including white,
- ❑ Bibles
- ❑ Colored markers or crayons
- ❑ Construction paper, all colors
- ❑ Glue or rubber cement
- ❑ Magazines
- ❑ Rulers
- ❑ Foam cups
- ❑ Tape
- ❑ Stapler, staples
- ❑ Yarn
- ❑ Glitter, optional
- ❑ Newsprint, optional
- ❑ Stickers, optional
- ❑ Straws or chenille stems, optional

MY OWN NOTES...
Use with lessons on...

52. Autograph Books

Students fold several pieces of 8-1/2" x 11" paper in half horizontally (short side to short side). Then staple twice on the middle of the fold. Decorate the front of their books with markers, pictures cut from magazines and glued on, or stickers. Students can have all their classmates sign it.

Option: Write "God Blesses Us With Friends" on the cover.

Use to reinforce lessons on friendship, loving one another, Jesus as friend, David and Jonathan.

53. Prayer Journals

Have students staple together seven pieces of paper (or more) and make a cover from construction paper. On each page, draw three columns. Label the first one: "Date." The second one: "Prayer Requests." The third one: "God's Answers." Students write out prayer needs and keep a record of answers.

Option: Use several whole or half sheets. Write a Scripture verse on some of the pages and illustrate them. Keep specific prayer requests on pages which have a picture and verse relating to those needs.

54. Recipe Book

Cover several half sheets with a construction paper cover. Decorate the covers and write "From the Kitchen Of . . ." or "To Your House from Our Classroom."

Suggestion: Have students bring a recipe card next week for other students to copy into their books. Give the books as gifts.

Can be used as Mother's Day gift or Christmas gift. If well-done, students could sell them to raise money for a special needs or missions offering.

55. Address Book

Make a book, any size, with 26 blank pages in it. Use a ruler to draw lines on the pages in their book. Write one letter of the alphabet at the top of each page, making spaces under each for names and addresses.

Option: Draw small pictures at the bottom of each page as decorations or use stickers.

Can be used as auxiliary to lessons on friends, family, the early church.

 PRAYER CARDS & HOLDER

56. Card Holder

Fold a strip of paper 8-1/2" wide and 3" high as shown. (One sheet of paper will make four holders.)

Fold up 1/2" from the bottom, then fold the width in half. Write: "Prayer Cards" or "God Answers Prayer" on the front of the holder and decorate by coloring with crayons or markers. Write prayer verses or requests and insert inside holder.

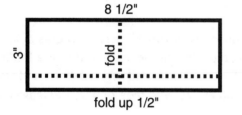

8 1/2"

3"

fold

fold up 1/2"

God Answers Prayer

front view

57. Prayer Cards

Cut as many 2" x 4" cards as desired. Decorate cards with personal art work or add stickers of praying hands or whatever is in the supply closet.

Write: "I'm praying for you" or a verse on each card. Students should also sign their prayer cards and give them to those for whom they are praying.

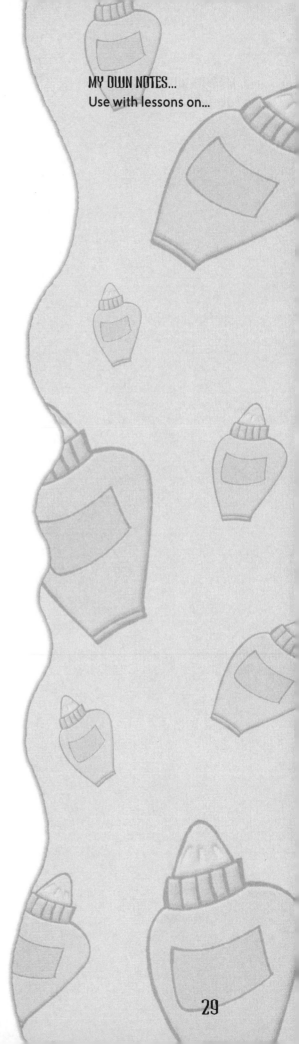

FLOWERS

58. Care Flowers

Cut two circles by tracing the bottom or top of a foam cup. Cut ten or more petals about 2" long and 1/2" wide. Then cut ten or more which are about 1-1/2" long by 1/4" wide. Round off the ends.

Glue the longer ones around one of the circles. Layer the shorter ones over the long ones. Glue the second circle over the ends of petals to cover them.

Roll one petal at a time around a pencil to curl them. Some will curl better than others, making the flower look more realistic. Make a stem from paper, a straw, or a chenille stem.

Option: Write Matthew 6:28-30 on the second circle.

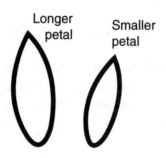

Longer petal   Smaller petal

59. Lilies

Cut a 4" square. Fold the square as shown. Place small pieces of tape in two or three places on the fold. Lily can be squeezed at the folded edges to look more round. A stem can be cut and colored green. Cut two leaves of any size (as in Craft 58 above) and tape or glue the leaves to stem.

Option: Write half of Luke 12:27 on each leaf.

Alternative: Make a bouquet of lilies, using straws as stems. Tie lilies together with yarn. Attach a tag to the yarn with the above verse or another verse of the student's choice.

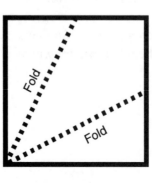

Fold
Fold

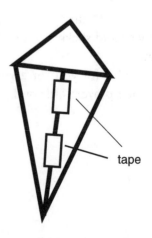

tape

60. Buttercups

Fold a 4" square in half twice to make a quartered square. Cut a shape similar to the one shown in Figure B.

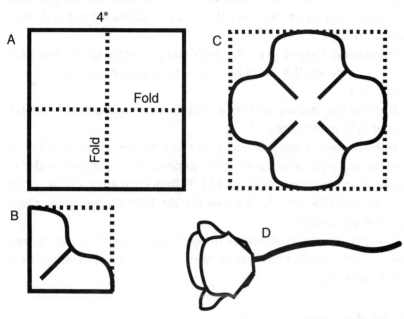

Next, make a cut to within 1/4" of the center. Unfold and color the flower. Overlap the petals at each slit and glue. Straws or chenille stems can be pushed through the middle for a stem, or a paper stem can be cut and glued to the flower.

Make a bouquet for Mother's Day; to encourage a sick child in the class, or send a bouquet home with a child whose parent is sick.

Hint: Make an easy flower-holder by rolling a piece of any type of paper into a cone shape and taping together. Insert flower stems through larger hole.

NOTES & STATIONERY

61. Fold 'n' Send Sheets

Half or whole sheets can be made into fold 'n' sends. Fold the sheet in thirds. Then, unfold and decorate the inside as desired with student art, stickers, or pictures cut from magazines and glued on. On the outside, draw address lines or make a box on middle section for address and in the upper left-hand corner for the return address.

Hint: Crayons are best to use because markers can show through the paper.

Suggestion: Grandparents are notoriously fond of grandchildren. Use as special gift so grandparents can use their grandchild's stationery when they write to their friends.

62. Note Pad

Cut pieces of paper into any size. Punch two holes at the top of the bundle and tie together with yarn. Yarn can also serve as a hanging loop. To decorate, place a small sticker at one corner of the top paper or write a verse in colored marker.

Suggestion: Verse can be the day's memory verse or another verse which reinforces the lesson truth which students look up in a concordance.

Option: Use rubber cement glue and glue the tops of the sheets together to form the note pad.

Option: Make a construction paper box for the sheets to set in. To make box, cut a piece of construction paper at least one inch wider on all sides than the paper. Make a fold 1/2" from each edge. Cut in 1/2" on one edge. Fold long, uncut piece over the shorter piece and glue or tape. Repeat on other sides.

Students may use notepads themselves or give as a gift. If well-done, students could sell them to raise money for a special needs or missions offering.

63. Stationery

Students cut or tear sheets of paper in half to make 5-1/2" x 8-1/2" sheets. Make a construction paper box as above to hold them. Decorate each sheet with colorful designs drawn with markers or crayons. Write a Bible verse on each sheet.

Envelopes: To make envelopes for the stationery sheets, fold an 8-1/2" x 11" piece of paper in half twice to make a quarter sheet. Use a ruler to mark cutting line as shown.

Cut along the line, then fold the sheet out flat. Fold in the sides as shown, then fold up the bottom flap and glue or tape. Fold down the top flap, but do not fasten. If desired, decorate the upper left corner of the envelopes to match the stationery.

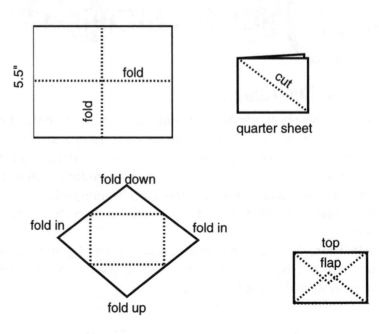

ENCOURAGERS

64. Promise Square

Cut an 8-1/2" square from paper. Fold each corner in to middle. Then fold back each point as shown.

Inside the middle of the square, write "God's Promises." On outside of each flap, have students write "Joy, Hope, God's Love, Peace." Have students look up these promises in their Bibles. Copy either the entire verse or just the reference under the flap that corresponds. Joy—Isaiah 55:12; John 15:11; John 16:22. Hope—Colossians 1:5; Colossians 1:27; 1 Peter 1:21. God's Love—John 3:16; 1 John 4:16; Romans 5: Mark 12:30-31. Peace—Philippians 4:7; Isaiah 57:19; John 14:27.

Encourage students to use their promise finders when they or someone else needs to be reminded of the wonderful promises God gives to His children.

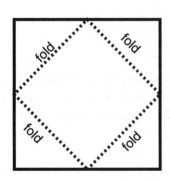

all corners folded
in toward middle

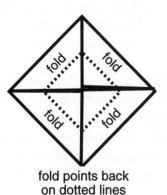

fold points back
on dotted lines

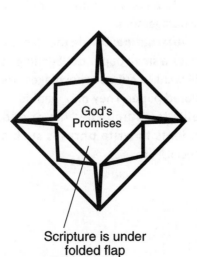

God's
Promises

Scripture is under
folded flap

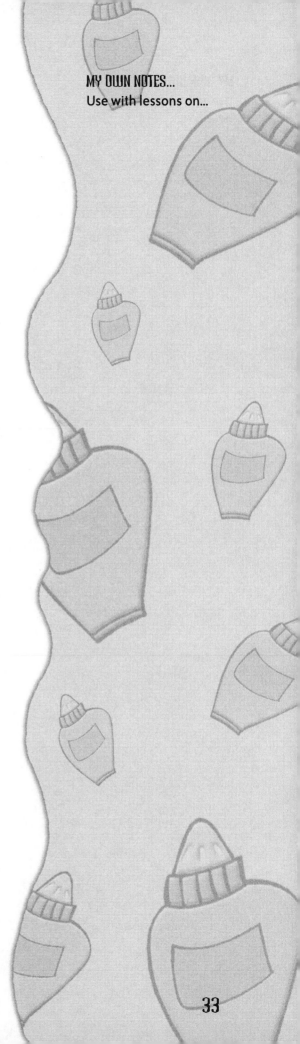

65. Psalm Windows

Cut a piece of paper in half to make two 4-1/4" x 11" strips. At the top of one strip, write: "Psalms to help me." Then, cut six windows as shown.

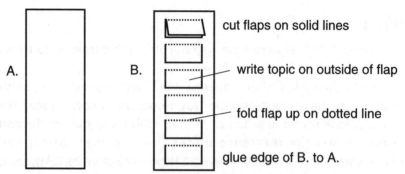

A.

B.

cut flaps on solid lines

write topic on outside of flap

fold flap up on dotted line

glue edge of B. to A.

Glue the two pieces together along the edges. On the outside of each window, write a topic such as: "When I'm lonely," "When I've failed," "When I'm sad," "When someone I love is ill," "When I am joyful," "When I want to praise God," etc. Then, have students look in Psalms and find a verse to match the topics. Write the Psalm on the inside of the window as the answer to the situation. (Some suggested Psalms: 4:7, 9:10, 27:1, 27:14, 31:24, 33:21, 37:3, 46:1, 51:6, 60:12, 71:5, 89:34.)

66. Friendship Quilt

Each student colors a design and writes encouraging words on a piece of paper. When finished, tape all the posters together to make a paper quilt. Display the quilt in your classroom or in the fellowship hall.

67. Mini-Quilt Heartwarmers

On a large piece of newsprint, mark off an area for each student. Students color their area with a design and friendship words. Give the quilt to a class member or elderly shut-in who has been ill or needs encouragement.

Alternative: Divide the class into groups of two or three. Each group makes a small paper quilt getting as elaborate as possible. Perhaps they will want to cut out snowflakes from white paper and mount that onto colored paper. They may want to make a stained glass effect. Take these quilts to church shut-ins or a local nursing home. Encourage the students to write phrases such as: "Jesus Loves You," or "You are Special," etc.

SIGNS & PLAQUES

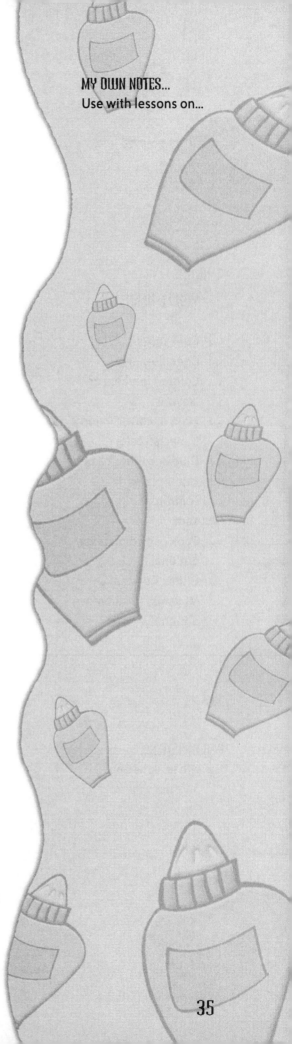

68. Room Signs

Cut out any size and shape from paper. Write a saying on it such as: "Trust God," "Jesus is the Reason," "God is My Answer," or "Jesus Loves Me." The words can be written in marker or crayon, or perhaps glue and glitter.

Options: Shadow the letters by using different colors. Write first letter of each word in glitter and dot the *i*'s with a spot of glitter. Cut letters from magazines and glue to sign. Outline the letters in small sticker dots or stars. Outline the sign in stickers, dots, stars, or glitter.

More Options: Cut shape-holes such as triangles, hearts, circles in a sheet of paper. Then glue this sheet on top of a piece of bright construction paper. In the shape-holes, write words or letters such as "J E S U S," or "For God So Loved the World," or "Psalm 23." Can also cut out letters from paper and glue into shape-holes.

HINT: Signs can be reinforced for strength by gluing the paper to a sheet of construction paper or a piece of brown paper bag. To make into a plaque, cover with a layer of glue and let dry. Glue yarn loop on the back as a hanger.

Use to reinforce almost any lesson truth.

69. Treasure Chest of Promises

Fold a piece of paper up 3" from the bottom and down 3" from the top. At the seam in the middle of page, students draw a lock and write _____'s Treasure of Bible Promises. On the inside of sheet, list some promises in the Bible.

Verse Suggestions: Psalm 138:7; Matthew 11:28; Isaiah 40:29; 1 John 2:25; 1 Thessalonians 4:16.

Option: Students may make a treasure chest for a parent or friend. Inside, have the students list things God provides for them, wonderful things God has done for them, etc.

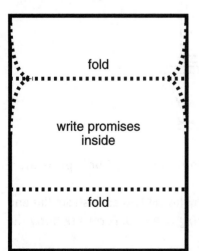

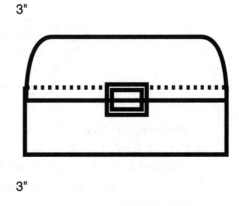

3

FRAMES

THINGS
YOU'LL NEED...

- ☐ Craft sticks
- ☐ Chenille stems
- ☐ Colored markers or crayons
- ☐ Plain or construction paper, all colors
- ☐ Glue or rubber cement
- ☐ Paper plates
- ☐ Foam cups
- ☐ Yarn
- ☐ Book of bird pictures, optional
- ☐ Glitter, optional
- ☐ Magnets, small pieces, optional

MY OWN NOTES...
Use with lessons on...

70. House Frame

Make a rectangular box shape, gluing the sticks at each corner. Make large dot of glue on top of each corner, flatten slightly, and let dry until almost hard. Make a second rectangular box shape while this is drying. Place this second box on top of the large glue dots. Do not squeeze together. Leave it slightly raised for a 3-D effect. Add one more layer to this following the same procedure.

Cut a piece of paper to fit the box shape. Have students write in colored markers: "As for me and my house, we will serve the LORD" (Josh. 24:15, KJV). Glue the paper to back of box shape so the words show through.

Then, make a V-shape the width of the rectangle at the bottom; turn it upside down and glue it to the outside of the last layer of sticks to add a roof to the house. A yarn loop can be attached to back of box for hanging.

Suggestion: Can be used to reinforce lessons on family, honoring parents, etc.

71. Ark Frame

Lay sticks out flat. Make a one layer frame as shown. Have students write their message on a piece of paper slightly larger than the size of the opening formed by the ark body. Glue the paper to the back of the ark so their message shows through.

Suggestion: Use with lesons on Noah's Ark, God's protection, God's Care, God's Faithfulness.

Option: Make Ark body larger by laying two craft sticks flat and gluing together by slightly overlapping one end. Form Ark body the same as above.

72. Nativity Star Frame

Make two triangles using four layers of sticks, glued one on top of the other. Place one triangle with the point upright on the table, then place the second triangle with the broad base about two-thirds of the way up the first triangle. Glue together to form a six-pointed star. Trace the shape of the middle of the two triangles on paper and cut out the shape. Write out Matthew 2:9 or Luke 2:11. Glue paper to back of frame.

Option: Students may outline their frames with star stickers or decorate by coloring with markers.

Suggestion: Can be used with lessons on creation, nature, etc.

73. Easter Frame

Make a 3-D cross by using the same procedure of layering as in the House Frame, but use two layers rather than three. Using colored paper, cut out a banner with wavy edges and write: "He has risen!" from Mark 16:6. Glue one end of the banner inside the cross where the two pieces join so it hangs out in a diagonal position. Or glue one end to the middle where the two pieces cross and let it extend out over the left end, gluing it down at the end of the cross piece.

BANKS

74. Square Bank

Build a box as in the House Frame, but make the box 10 sticks deep. Glue sticks across the back of the box. Trace and cut a piece of paper to fit the top of the box. Cut a slit in the middle of the paper about 1/4" wide and 2" long. Glue the paper to the top of the box.

Suggestion: Before gluing the paper to the top of bank, write a verse with markers or decorate with markers or stickers.

Use to reinforce lessons on giving, the early church and how they gave, and the Widow's Mite.

75. Bank with Lid

Make a bank frame as above, but don't put a paper lid on it. Glue four sticks together at the corners to form a square. Spread glue around the entire square, lay sticks across until the square is filled in. When glue is dry, have students decorate lid with markers or stickers.

For a handle, make a U-shape from a chenille stem. Tape or glue both ends of the stem to the top of the bank lid.

ORNAMENTS

76. Glitter Sticks

Write in marker on both sides of a craft stick "Jesus is Lord." Spread glue on the top and bottom of the stick and sprinkle on glitter. Glue a yarn loop to top of stick.

77. Glitter Cross

Glue two sticks together to form a cross. Write "He is Risen" on either the cross piece or the vertical piece in glue. Sprinkle glitter over the glue and shake off excess. Attach a loop of yarn.

78. Yarn-Wrap Cross

Wrap two craft sticks with yarn and glue the end of the yarn to the stick to secure it. Form a cross and wrap yarn around the middle to hold it together. Leave a loop for hanging.

79. Stars

Glue three sticks together in a triangle. Then make a second triangle. Place one triangle upside down about two-thirds of the way up the first triangle. Glue together to form a six-sided star. Cover with glue and sprinkle with glitter. Add a yarn loop to the top of one triangle.

80. Yarn-Wrap Star

Wrap six craft sticks in yarn. (Star will be more colorful if each stick is a different color.) Form triangle and glue together. Place broad base of one yarn-wrapped triangle over the first triangle (as in #79) and use yarn to tie the two together into a star. Tie a loop around one point of a triangle.

Option: Turn any ornament into a refrigerator magnet by gluing a piece of magnet strip to back instead of adding the yarn loop.

81. Prayer Tree

Glue three sticks to piece of white paper vertically to form tree trunk. Write on the sticks, _____'s Prayer Tree. Add sticks as shown for branches.

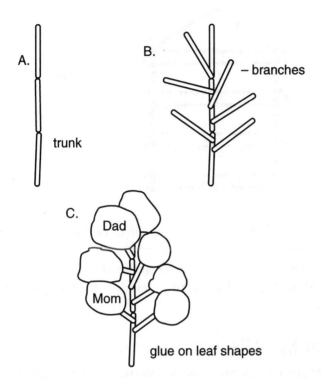

A. trunk

B. – branches

C. Dad Mom

glue on leaf shapes

Make cloud-like shapes out of green construction paper as leaf cover for each branch. Write a prayer on each "leaf cloud" such as: "Leaders of our country," "Mom, Dad, Bobby is ill," etc. Glue onto branches.

TRIVETS & HANGERS

82. Trivet

Lay 12 craft sticks side-by-side. Cover one side of another craft stick with glue. Lay it across the 12 sticks, about 1" from edge. Repeat at other end. When glue has dried, decorate trivet.

Suggestions: Cut three 1-foot lengths of yarn, each a different color. Spread glue onto trivet in a design. Put one piece of yarn onto glue and press down in design. Add more glue and the second piece of yarn. Repeat for the last piece of yarn.

Can be given as a gift to Mother or Grandmother.

83. Scripture Hanger

Choose a verse to write on craft sticks. Lay out one stick for each word. Write word on each stick with marker. Cut two pieces of yarn about 2 feet long. Tie a length of yarn around one end of each stick, leaving about 2 inches between sticks as shown.

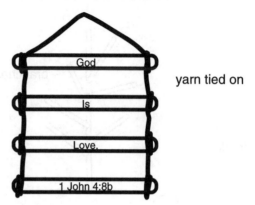

yarn tied on

Repeat for the other end of sticks. Cut a 6" length of yarn and tie one end to each end of the top stick.

Option: Scripture Magnet. Make the hanger as above, but substitute two pieces of magnet strip in place of the yarn length. Glue magnet strips to back of top stick.

84. Verse or Story Hanger

Cut a strip of any kind of paper. Write a verse, promise, or prayer on it. Glue a stick at top and bottom and add a yarn length to hang. Decorate with glitter or markers.

Option: Make a hanger as above. Instead of writing on the paper, draw scenes of current Bible lesson or a favorite Bible story.

MOBILES

Make the mobiles below to correspond with lessons on Creation, Noah, or Nature.

Basic directions:

Draw around the bottom of a foam cup on a paper plate and cut out the hole in center. Punch three holes at least 1/2" away from edge of this center hole. Loop a length of yarn through holes and pull up. Tie together with at least a 6" loop for hanging.

Punch holes around the edge of the paper plate. Hang various lengths of yarn from holes. Have students make birds, fish, or animals as described below. Tie these creations to the yarn lengths.

Option: On the paper plate, write: "God created the world (animals, fish, birds, etc.)" or "God's creation is wonderful."

85. Birds

Cut out two triangles and fan-fold them. Glue the largest end of the fan-folded triangles to each side of a craft stick. Make a fan-folded tail and glue to end of stick. Use markers to add eyes and make a beak by rolling a small piece of paper together and taping to front of stick. Sticks can be colored to represent different types of birds.

Option: Bring a book of bird pictures to class so students can have several ideas of what kind of bird to make and color. Glue several sticks together lengthwise for larger birds.

fan-folded triangle tail

rolled paper beak

craft stick body

glue to craft stick

fan-folded triangle wings

86. Fish

Cut out four small hearts. On one end of a craft stick, draw eyes and a mouth. About halfway toward the other end of the stick, glue the point of one heart to each side of the stick. Point should be toward the face. On the other end of the stick, glue the points of a heart facing outward on each side for the tail.

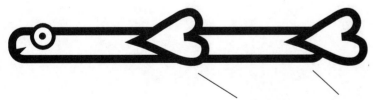

glue hearts on each side of fish

Can also reinforce lessons such as Feeding the 5,000, Miracle of the Great Catch of Fish, Tax Money in the Mouth of Fish, etc.

87. Mice

Make mice as in #20 Mouse Bookmark (Chapter 1). Cut out a gray circle and fold it in half to make the mouse's body. Glue over craft stick.

Cut a 6" length of gray or pink yarn and glue to one end of a craft stick for mouse's tail. Cut six 1/2" lengths of pink, black, white, or gray yarn (or chenille stem) and glue three to each side of stick for whiskers. Draw an eye on each side and glue on a small triangle of pink paper for the nose.

Cut two ovals for ears. Pinch one end of each to make a partial fold. Glue the pinched ends of the ears on the mouse, just above the eyes. (Ears will point upward.) Add two small pink ears.

88. Dachshunds

Cut two long ears and four 2" to 3" long legs from brown paper and a tail of brown or white. Glue ears to each side of a craft stick at one end. Glue the tail to the other end. Then glue the four legs along the bottom edge of the stick, two on each side. At the end with the ears, draw an eye on each side of the stick and put a black spot on the very tip of the stick for a nose.

Option: Give students craft sticks, glue, markers, and construction paper. Let their imaginations take over. They will create some wonderful and whimsical animals or people.

More Options: Turn any of the creatures into refrigerator magnets by adding features to only one side of the craft stick. On the other side, glue two small bits of magnet strip.

FOAM CUP CRAFTS

4

CHARIOTS

89. Bible Times Chariot

Cut a foam cup in half vertically. Poke two holes opposite each other in the middle of the sides for the axle and insert half a straw along the bottom curve of the cup. Leave open side of cup up. Cut four wheels out of construction paper. Glue two together for strength. Poke small hole in middle and slide over ends of straw. Color remaining half-straw brown and glue to front of chariot as the center yoke to which the horses would be attached.

(Note: Although chariots had only two wheels, if you desire stability, make four holes and four wheels.)

Option: Elijah's Chariot of Fire can be made by cutting flames from orange and red paper. Glue the flames to the chariot.

Option: Make Phillip and Eunuch chariot as above. Add gold or silver glitter on outside of chariot.

People: Make cylinder figures by cutting two 4" squares of paper. Roll together and tape. Draw faces on each and hair or beards as desired. Tape or glue into the chariot. Beards can be made by cutting an appropriately sized piece of paper from black or brown construction paper. Make several vertical slits, but leave at least 1/4" at the top. Use a pencil to curl the paper slits. Glue in place.

CRITTERS

90. Animals

For a general figure, use craft sticks for legs and necks. Use one foam cup for the body and another for the head. See illustration. Add construction paper features such as ears and tails to create animals.

paper cup   craft sticks

THINGS YOU'LL NEED...

- ☐ Foam cups
- ☐ Construction paper, all colors
- ☐ Craft sticks
- ☐ Glue or rubber cement
- ☐ Markers or crayons, all colors
- ☐ Paper plates
- ☐ Yarn
- ☐ Hole punch, optional
- ☐ Pencils, new and unsharpened, optional

MY OWN NOTES...

Use with lessons on...

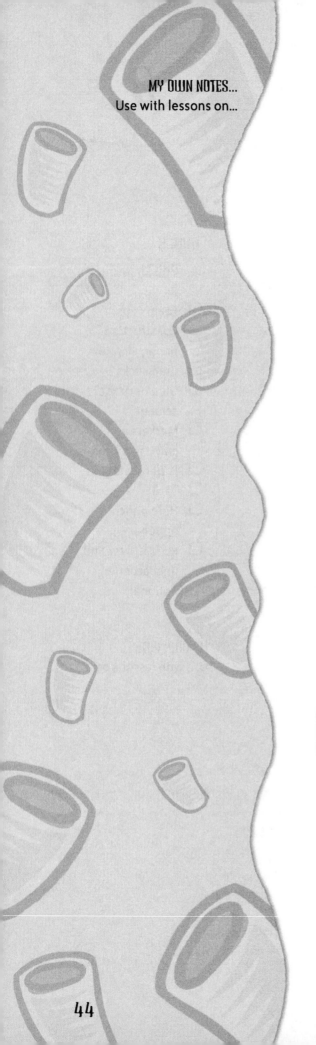

91. Animal Noses

Students can create noses to wear by cutting, coloring, and gluing extra features onto a foam cup. Poke two holes in opposite sides at least 1/2" in from the cup rim. Use yarn to tie onto head.

Pig snout. Color the cup all pink and make the flat end of the cup all black.

Cow nose. Color big black or brown spots all around cup. Make end of cup all black.

Mouse. Color cup gray. Color end of cup pink. Add some yarn or construction paper whiskers to the sides of the cup by the flat end.

92. Animal Heads

Let students use their imaginations to create animal heads. Turn foam cups upside down so opening is on the table. Then add any of the following.

Dog. Cut long floppy ears from colored construction paper. Glue onto sides of foam cup, hanging larger, bulbous end down. Color big brown eyes and a nose on the front of the cup. Glue on yarn whiskers and a red tongue cut from construction paper.

Cat. Cut short stand-up ears (like small triangles.) Color a dark gray or black nose and mouth. Add whiskers.

Giraffe. Color cup yellow and add brown spots. Color eyes and nose. Add short ears and two short horns. Glue two craft sticks end to end and place "head" on top of the "neck."

Elephant. Cut out big gray ears and a trunk from construction paper. Glue these onto the sides and end of the cup, then color eyes and a mouth.

GIFTS

93. Pencil Cup

Glue a few lengths of yarn around the top edge of a foam cup. Write a verse in colored markers. Or, cut a piece of construction paper to wrap around the cup. Write a verse or a saying on it and glue it on. Or, glue it on first at the rim of the cup, glue yarn around the rim, and let the paper hang straight down like a vertical banner.

Suggestion: Buy pencils and give to pastor or a parent or a teacher.

94. Planter

Punch holes around top edge of foam cup with hole punch or a sharp pencil. Cut at least two 10" lengths of yarn to fit in each hole. Tie yarn through holes. Gather the yarn at bottom of cup and tie together with a shorter length of yarn.

Add three pieces of yarn about 6" long, as shown, and tie at top to form hanger.

punch holes

yarn hanger

tie here

Option: Provide potting soil and small plant for each child to complete the planter and take home as a gift for Mom or Grandma.

95. Pick~a~Promise Bouquet

Decorate a cup with markers or crayons. Stickers may also be added. Cut tulip shapes from colored construction paper (rounded sides and bottom with 3 to 4 jagged peaks across the top) about 2" wide and 2" high. Glue the tulips to craft sticks. Then, write a promise on the stick such as: "Pick up toys," "Help with dinner," "Fold towels," "Read to brother," etc.

Encourage students to give Mom the promise bouquets and to carry out the promises.

Use with lessons on honoring and obeying parents.

TEXTURE PICTURES

96. Texture Cross

Foam from foam cups makes an interesting texture when broken into pieces. Cut any size cross from paper bag, brown construction paper, or craft sticks. Break up a foam cup and glue the pieces to the cross.

97. I'm Somebody Special Plaque

Have students write their names with colored markers or pencils in large letters on a bright piece of construction paper. Glue broken pieces of foam cup onto the lettering. When finished gluing, have students write in marker some words that describe themselves (smart, helpful, follower of Jesus. . .) or words they want to be descriptive of their lives (courageous, obedient, loving, etc.).

Option: Drip glue on the foam pieces and then sprinkle with glitter.

98. Rainbow

Cut a paper plate in half. On the outside of both pieces, draw thick black lines to make the seven sections of rainbow colors. Then, color the outside of seven cups with bright colors; break or tear them up. Glue the torn bits to the rainbow, making sure to keep one color inside each set of lines. When finished gluing, staple the two plate halves together and add a loop at top for hanging.

WINDSOCKS

99. Braided Windsock

An upside-down cup forms the base for this windsock. Poke two holes in the bottom of cup and add a yarn length for a hanger.

Then punch nine holes around bottom edge of cup. On the cup, write: "God keeps His promises." For streamers, cut three equal lengths of one color yarn. Braid these three and use as one streamer. Then, make eight more streamers in different colors, enough to fit in all the holes.

100. Spring Windsock

Make Braided Windsock. For streamers, attach bunches of yarn (do not braid) of pastel colors about ten lengths to a bunch. Have several colors in each bunch.

MAGAZINE OR CATALOG CRAFTS

5

CARDS, BOOKLETS, GREETINGS

101. Special Messages

Cut several sizes and colors of letters out of magazines to make encouraging messages. Glue the messages onto a half-sheet of paper.

Suggested messages: "God loves you and I do, too." "You are special." "Thank you for praying for me."

Suggestion: When glue is dry, give or mail message-notes to someone.

Suggestion: Send messages to a missionary family your church supports. Combine with other craft projects such as notepads, scroll plaques, or scrapbooks and make up a special gift that will encourage both the adults and children in the family. Bring the names and ages and a picture of the family to class so students can feel a personal connection to them.

102. Mother's or Father's Day Card

Fold a sheet of construction paper in half. Glue a message (and a picture, if desired) from cut-out magazine letters to front of card. Add a handwritten message inside accompanied by a drawing (or magazine picture) of one of their favorite activities with that parent.

Option: A sheet of white paper can be folded to match the fold of the construction paper and glued inside to make the message stand-out.

Option: Have students bring a picture of themselves to add to the card. Make a round cut-out on the front by tracing the bottom of a foam cup; cut it out. Student's picture will show through when mounted inside the card.

103. Praise Wall Hanging

Cut a strip of any type paper, about 3" wide and any length. Cut out letters to form words, and glue them vertically down the length of paper.

Enhance the wall hangings with a glitter or sticker border or have students punch holes down both sides and lace one or two colors of yarn through them.

Ideas: "Praise the Lord." "Jesus is Lord." "No one loves me like Jesus." "I will serve my Lord."

THINGS YOU'LL NEED...

- ❏ Magazines and catalogs, four-color
- ❏ Glue or rubber cement
- ❏ Hole punch
- ❏ Markers or crayons, all colors
- ❏ Paper plates
- ❏ Plain and construction paper, all colors
- ❏ Staplers, staples
- ❏ Foam cups
- ❏ Yarn
- ❏ Glitter, optional
- ❏ Stickers, optional
- ❏ Pictures of the children in the class, optional

MY OWN NOTES...
Use with lessons on...

104. Flip-Card Greetings

Cut three pieces of construction paper into quarters. (Fold each piece of paper lightly into half and then half again; cut on fold lines.) Punch two holes in top of each piece. Tie all 12 pieces together loosely with yarn. Fill the greeting booklet with encouragements such as "Hang in there." "Good Job!" "Get well soon." "You can do it." Use magazines to cut out appropriate pictures such as medicine ad, person winning race, flowers, etc. Glue pictures to pages of booklet. May also cut out letters of first word. Add an appropriate verse to each page.

Use to reinforce lessons on encouragement, caring, love.

105. Cheers For You, Poms

Cut 1" x 8" strips from magazine pages and staple together in the middle. Make a handle by folding a 4" square of white paper in half and then in half again. Write: "WAY TO GO!" "YOU CAN DO IT!" or "I'M CHEERING FOR YOU!" on the handle. Staple to each side of the middle of the magazine strip bundle.

Give cheers to someone to encourage them.

106. Pop-out Card

Fold a bright piece of construction paper in half to make a card. On the inside, tape a flat pom at bottom of page. Pom will pop out when card is opened.

Option: To make a Pop-Up Card, take a white sheet of paper, write a message on it with colorful markers. Fold into fan, staple in middle and leave flat. Tape, glue or staple the flat fan inside the construction paper near the fold at the top of the card. When card is opened, fan can be unfolded to stand up.

FAN~FOLDS

107. Starburst

Make two large fan-folded angel wing ornaments. Pull ends of long edges together by folding in the middle of the long side, and tape or staple ends together to make a colorful starburst.

Option: Tape streamers of paper decorated with glitter to the back of the starburst so that they extend below it. Streamers should be in proportion to the size of the starburst, but approximately 2" to 3" wide by 18" to 24" inches long. Write any message on the streamers.

108. Angel Wings Ornament

Select a brightly colored page from magazine and tear it out. Fan-fold the page and staple in the middle. Then, fan out the folds a little and add yarn for hanging.

Option: Angel Wing Mobile. Cut several magazine pages into quarters. Fan-fold and staple each piece in the middle. Make as many angel wings as desired and hang from a half paper plate. Decorate plate half with markers or stickers. Write a verse on the plate such as: Exodus 33:2a; Numbers 20:16; Matthew 1:20; Matthew 4:11b; Isaiah 6:2.

Option: Wings can also be made from plain paper or colored construction paper.

Use with lessons on: Jacob's Ladder, Birth of Jesus, After Jesus' temptation in desert, Isaiah's vision.

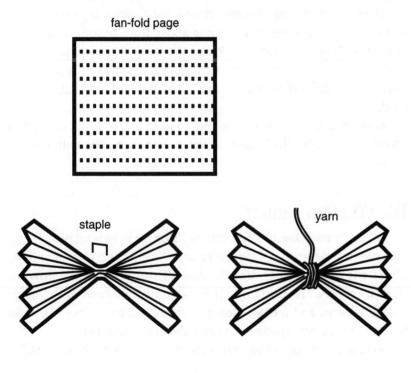

109. Sun, Moon, and Stars Mobile

Make a large starburst from yellow construction paper as the sun. Punch eight to ten holes in bottom edge of starburst from which to hang moon and stars. Use quartered magazine pages to make smaller starbursts. Add glitter to folded edges of starbursts and hang from sun with yarn. Make a half-moon from 1/2 magazine page. Follow directions for fan-folded angel wings. Punch a hole in one end of each ornament and hang from large starburst with different lengths of yarn.

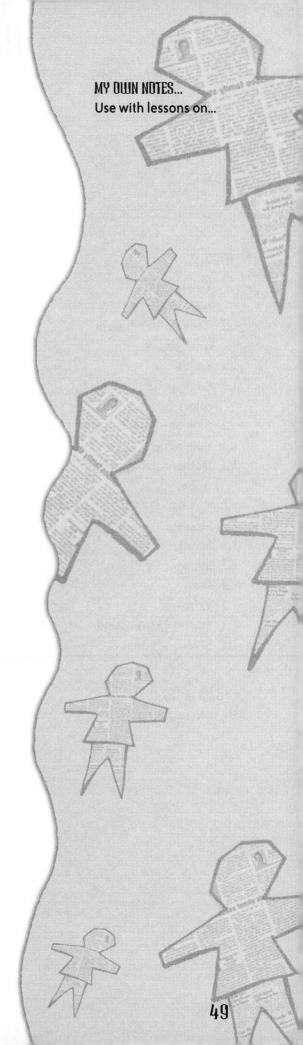

6

NEWSPRINT FOR FREEZER WRAP PAPER CRAFTS

BANNERS

110. Centipede Banner

Have students stand together at a long strip of paper. Have students trace their hands on a long strip of newsprint. (Fingers should point toward bottom edge.) Make some of the handprints a little above or below others but be sure all are touching. If you have only a few students, have them trace their hands several times.

Have students color fingers. Draw a head with a big smile at one end of centipede. Write this heading above the handprints in center of banner: "Lots of Reasons to Praise the Lord." Have students write praise phrases on each hand such as: "God is love." "Jesus is the answer." "I will serve only you, Lord." "Let us go into the house of the Lord."

Option: Students may write their names along top of centipede handprints. Display the banner in the church foyer. Use with lessons on praise.

111. Creation Banner

Students trace their handprints or fistprints in several places on a long piece of newsprint. Place at various heights and turn in various directions on the paper. Use the hand/fistprints to make flowers, clouds, animals, fish, birds, etc. They can trace their hand with fingers spread upward and part of their arm to make a tree. They can draw flowers, clouds, etc. inside the open palm of the handprint.

Across the top of the banner write "God's Wonderful Creation."

112. Honor God Everywhere Banner

Hang a long piece of paper on the wall or give each student a 2 foot x 2 foot square of paper. Provide colored markers. Tell students to illustrate ways and places they can honor, serve, or obey God. Write at the top of the banner: "I Can Honor God Everywhere." If students do individual squares, place them together as one long banner when they are done.

Suggestions: Students may draw a large church on the banner and then individually draw themselves singing, giving, learning in class. Inside a school, students may want to draw themselves being respectful and helpful, studying quietly. Inside a home, students might draw themselves helping, praying, reading Bible, having family Bible study, obeying parents, etc.

113. Personal Banner

Students each draw themselves (or have someone else trace their outline), filling the whole height of a long piece of paper. Have them write their names below or above their pictures. Have them write at the top: "I'm important to God because . . . ." Then they add their own identifiers to complete the phrase.

Ideas: God created me. God loves me. I obey Jesus. I can help others know Jesus as Savior. I am fearfully and wonderfully made.

 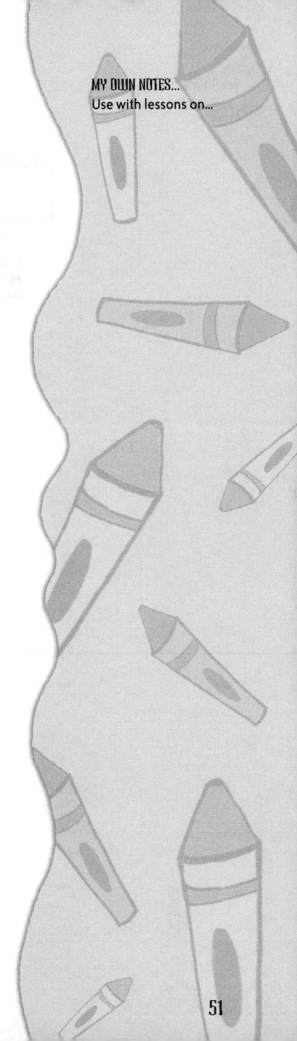

GARLANDS

114. Cross Garland

Cut a long strip of paper—up to 3 feet long, about 4 inches high. Fan-fold the strip along the width. Then, cut a cross shape being careful not to cut along the fold at the crossbars.

Unfold and color as desired. (To make a really long garland, students may each cut one, and then tape them all together.)

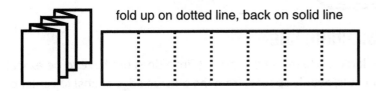

fold up on dotted line, back on solid line

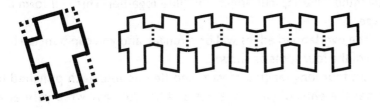

115. Friends Garland

Cut a strip of newsprint at least 1" taller than their hands and as wide as desired, up to 3 feet long. Fan-fold the strip, making the folds no wider than the student's hand. Then, trace handprint onto the top fold, letting fold on each side be part of the sides of their hand. Cut out hand and unfold into a long strip of hands.

Students may have their classmates sign on the handprints. Encourage them to put garland in their room at home, to remind them to pray for their friends

116. God Cares Garland

Cut a strip of white paper 6 inches high and up to 3 feet long. Fan-fold the strip. On top folded piece, draw a shape as shown.

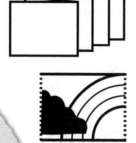

Half of shape will be a rainbow and the other half a cloud. When cut, unfold the garland and color the rainbows. On the clouds at each end of garland, write: "God Always Cares."

Encourage students to hang their garlands up at home and to remember that God is always present, even in the cloudy times of our lives.

KITES

117. Parachute Kite

Cut a large circle from newsprint. (Circle does not have to be exact.) Make four cuts, evenly spaced, from the outside edge almost to center of circle. Draw scenes of God's creation or write out Scripture verses on the parachute. Overlap cut edges and glue together. This will form a cup-shape.

The overlapped edges will be stronger, and you can punch a hole in each of the four spots as shown.

Cut four long lengths of yarn and tie one into each punched hole. Gather the ends of yarn together and tie. You may wrap yarn around straws or craft sticks as above. Tie an end to the 4 parachute strings that are tied together.

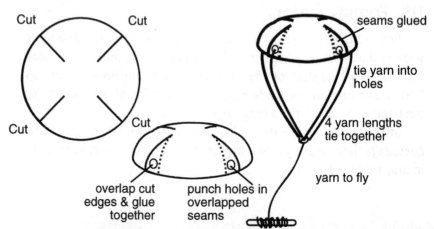

Cut   Cut

seams glued

tie yarn into holes

Cut   Cut

4 yarn lengths tie together

yarn to fly

overlap cut edges & glue together   punch holes in overlapped seams

118. Praise Kite

Place two straws at right angles to each other and glue together to make a foundation for the kite. Lay on newsprint and cut out a diamond shape, slightly larger than the straws. Decorate kite paper diamond with markers, using praise phrases or Scripture verses.

Fold a 1/2" to 1" seam on each side.

Glue or staple seam, leaving room to thread yarn through.

Make a "needle" to guide yarn through seams by cutting a 3-inch piece of straw. Lace yarn through straw "needle" and tape at the end.

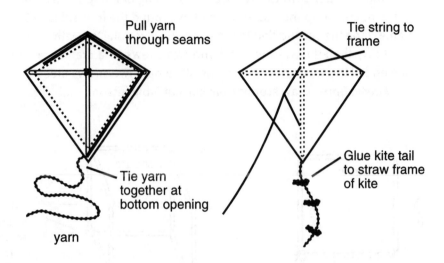

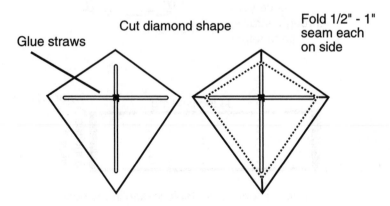

Then, pull yarn through the kite seams. Tie the ends.

Tape or glue diamond shape to frame. Make a tail from yarn and strips of paper. Tie, glue, or tape to frame.

For string to fly kite, wrap several feet of yarn around two straws or a craft stick. Tie one end of the yarn to kite.

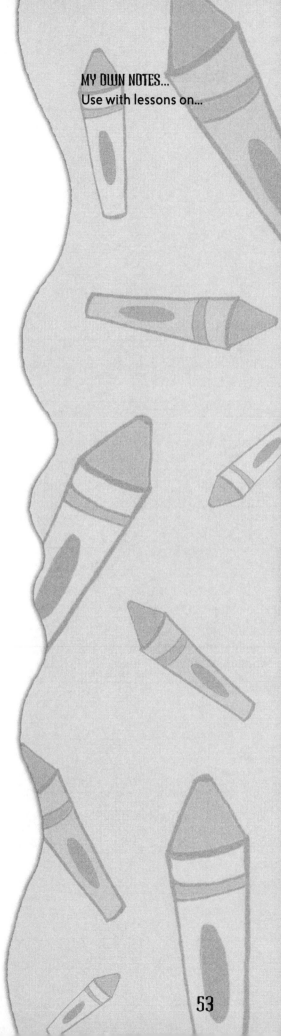

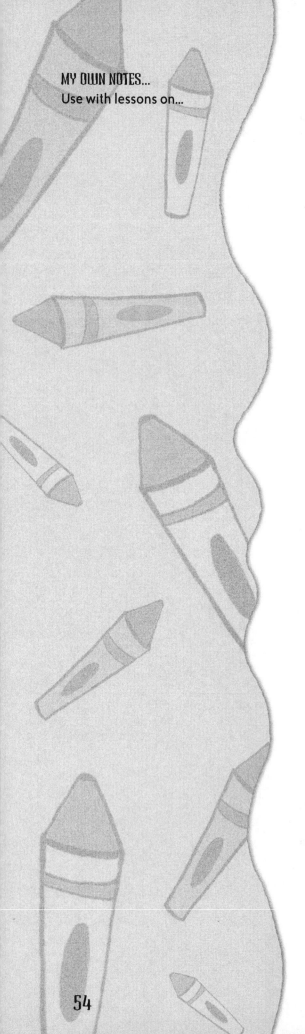

119. Box Kite

Lace a 35" length of yarn through four straws and tie ends together. This will form a square. Make a second square. At each of the four corners of the two squares, attach a straw as shown. This will form a box.

Hint: Wrap some tape around end of yarn so it will lace easier.

Cut a piece of newsprint 8" x 34". Mark off four squares as shown, leaving 1" flap at each end.

Attach paper strip to straw frame by taping one flap to any straw in the frame. Wrap the paper completely around the four sides of the frame. Tape the second flap to the same straw you started with.

To fly the kite, wrap yarn around two straws or a craft stick. Tie one end of the yarn to a corner of the kite where two straws meet.

Suggestions: Draw scenes from current Bible lesson.

1.

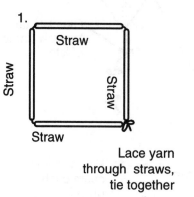

Lace yarn through straws, tie together

2.

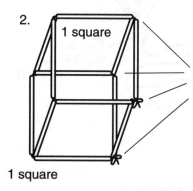

1 square

Attach 4 straws, at each corner o both sid

1 square

3.

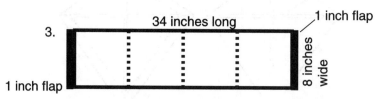

34 inches long

1 inch flap

1 inch flap

8 inches wide

Draw four scenes from Bible lesson in the boxes

4.

5.

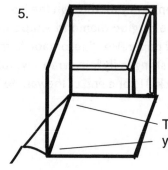

Tie 2 corners t yarn for flying

STUFFED SHAPES

120. Promise Rainbow

Cut two rainbow shapes from newsprint, leaving an extra inch on each side. (Trace around a paper plate and then cut out the circle. Fold in half and cut apart.) Color both sides of each half with crayons or markers. Tape rainbow shapes together by overlapping the extra inch, leaving a large opening to stuff paper into. Crumple up newsprint or magazine pages and fill the rainbow. When rainbow is full, tape or glue open edge and seal closed.

Leave extra inch around
rainbow shape

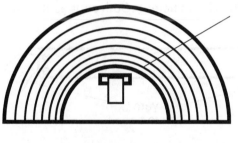

slit for promise strip
leave part of strip
hanging out
to tear off when read

blessings or promises written
on roll up strip

Option: Cut a strip of newsprint about 2" wide and at least 2 feet long. Have students write promises from God on the strips. The Psalms contain many promises. Or, students may want to make up their own statements such as: "God promises to care for me." "I believe all of God's Word." "I have eternal life."

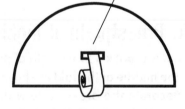

Roll the strips around a straw or pencil. Cut a slit about 2" long in the front of rainbow. Insert the rolled up promises into the slit, leaving the first promise partially unrolled, as illustrated.

Students can keep their promise rainbows or give to a friend.

121. Hearts of Love

Cut out two large hearts, color, and assemble as in the rainbows above. Make a strip to insert into the heart. However, on this strip, list love verses from the Bible.

ARMOR OF GOD

Ephesians 6:11-17

122. Fruit of the Spirit Mobile

Begin by making a stuffed rectangle, circle, or tree as in Activity 120 and write: "Fruit of the Spirit, Galatians 5:22-23." Then draw two each of nine fruits such as apples, oranges, bananas, etc. Glue and stuff them after writing one of the fruit on it. Hang the fruits from the larger shape using yarn and a stapler.

123. Belt of Truth

Students measure their waists with a piece of yarn, then cut the yarn and lay it on a piece of newsprint. Cut newsprint the same length as yarn and about 9 inches wide. Then fold the newsprint longways in thirds to make a stronger belt. Punch two holes in both ends as shown.

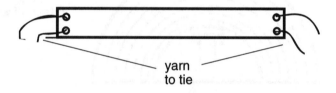

yarn
to tie

Thread two 10" lengths of yarn through the punched holes and tie to the paper belt. This will serve as the tie for their belt.

Suggestion: On back of belt, write: "I serve the God of truth, not the master of lies."

124. Breastplate of Righteousness

Cut a 1 foot x 3 foot length of paper. Fold the paper in half and cut a V in the middle of the fold as shown.

Decorate the breastplate with glitter and color with markers. On front, write: "RIGHTEOUSNESS." Breastplate will slip over head and need not be fastened.

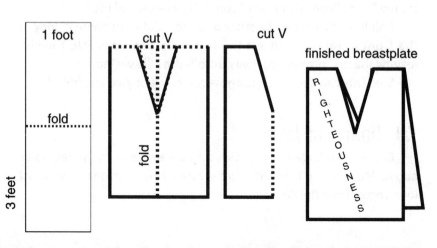

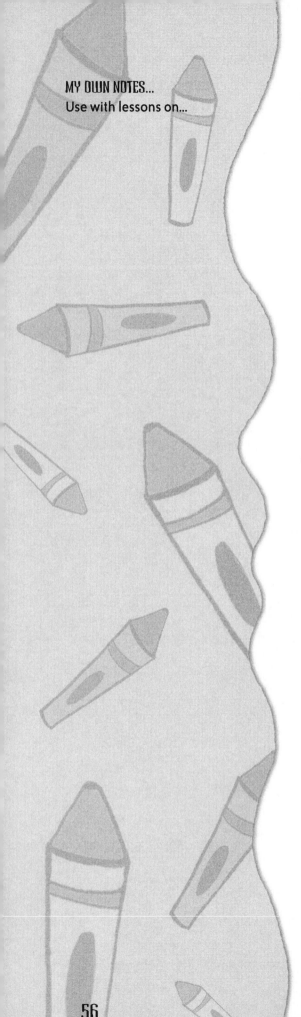

125. Footwear

Measure and cut two pieces of newsprint each 8" x 12". Fold each piece in half and turn to the side, so you have a paper folded 4" tall and 11" wide. With the folded edge facing upward, cut as follows: Begin 4" from the left and cut down 2", then turn scissors and cut across the back as shown.

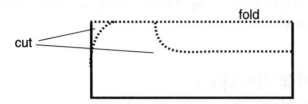

Left edge of paper is the front of footwear. Round off the point of the left edge slightly with scissors. Write: "Gospel of Peace" on the toe of footwear and decorate. Make two and tape onto feet at the back as shown.

126. Shield of Faith

Cut a shield from a piece of construction paper in a shape similar to the one illustrated.

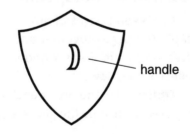

Trace this shape onto newsprint and cut out. On the newsprint shield, write: "FAITH" in glue. Sprinkle on gold or silver glitter.

Staple the newsprint shield to the construction paper one, leaving an opening. Stuff some crumpled newsprint into shield, then staple the opening shut. Cut a strip of newsprint 4" x 8". Fold in half to make handle 2" x 8" and tape to back of shield for a handle.

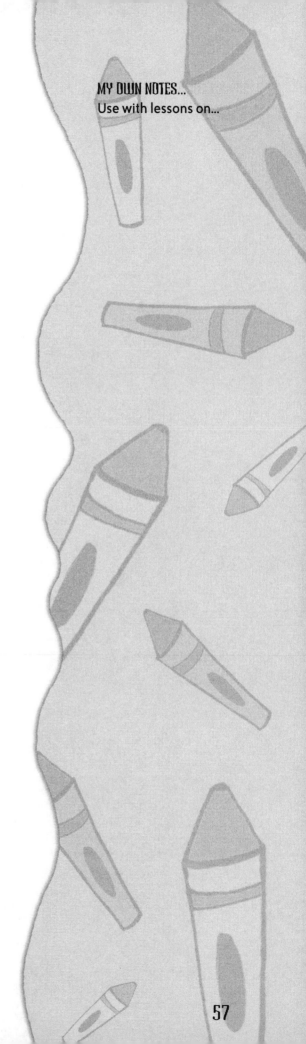

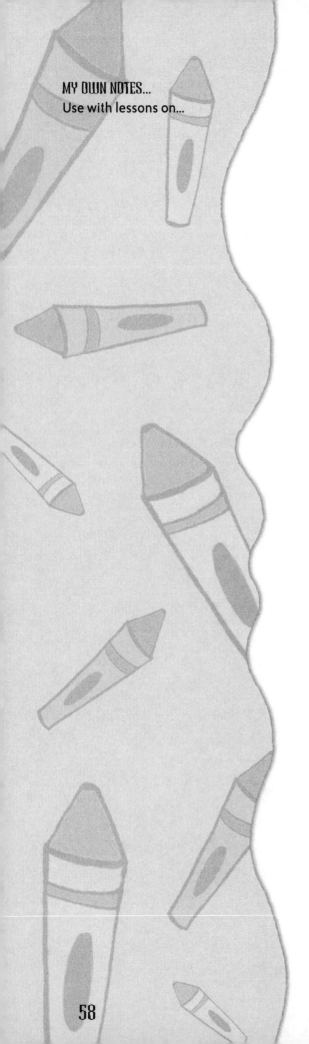

127. Helmet of Salvation

Cut two V shapes. The width at widest part of V should be about 12 inches. Turn so that the point of the ∧ faces upward. Fold point over slightly and glue, tape, or staple. (This rounds off the point.) Leave sides open, but overlap the two outer points and glue, tape, or staple each side. Leave the bottom open to fit over student's head. Decorate helmet with glitter. Write "SALVATION" down the middle of the helmet front with markers or glue.

128. Sword of the Spirit

Fold a 30" x 20" strip of paper longways about five times to make a long, thin, sword blade. Glue or staple the long edge. Make a handle from yellow construction paper. Cut two cross shapes. Glue to each side of blade and glue or staple two handles together at the end. With glue, write "WORD OF GOD" down the blade and sprinkle gold or silver glitter in the glue. On the handle, write BIBLE.

Suggestion: If students have made the entire suit of armor, have them model their creations in front of the congregation. They may recite the verse about each piece from Ephesians 6:11-17.

BOOKS

129. Nature Scrapbook

Cut several pages of any size as long as they are the same size. Staple the pages together and decorate the cover. Write on front: "Treasures from God's Wonderful Creation." Encourage students to collect leaves, flowers, etc.

Option: Use the hole punch to make two holes on the left-hand edge. Use yarn to tie the pages together instead of stapling.

130. Footprint Book

Students trace their own footprint and cut out several. Staple all of them together at the heel.

Idea: On the first footprint, write: "I Will Follow Jesus." Encourage students to fill their books with ways they can follow Jesus and ways they actually do follow Him in their daily lives.

PAPER BAG CRAFTS

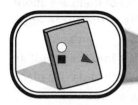

7

BOOK COVERS

131. Bible Cover

Cut open a paper bag and lay flat. Open a Bible and place it on the bag. Trace around Bible, leaving an extra 2" at the top and bottom and 3 at each side. Cut out. If your paper bag has printing on it, make sure that side stays toward the Bible, and not the outside.

Fold paper up 2" from bottom and down 2" from top. Place a few pieces of tape along the edges to hold in the flaps. Then place opened Bible on the book cover and fold in the sides 2" or 2-1/2". Slip cover of Bible into the flaps and close. (It gets tighter at the sides when closed.)

If using crayon or stickers to decorate Bible cover, leave it on the Bible. However, marker colors or glue may seep through the paper. So, take cover off Bible before using markers or glue.

Idea: Write on front of cover: "My Sword of the Spirit," or "Holy Bible." Try writing the words with one color marker, then again, with another color.

Option: This craft can be made and used to cover any sized book. Suggest students cover their school books with a new cover every week and have different verses or pictures.

BRAIDED PAPER

132. Friendship Ring

Cut three strips, each 1/2" wide and about 6" long. Fold in half longways and braid as shown in Activity 134. Stop braiding when ring is long enough to fit around a friend's finger easily. Cut and glue ends (or staple). Form a ring and glue or tape together.

133. Headband

Cut paper strips 3 feet long and 1 inch wide. Make each strip a different color. Fold in half and braid as above. Place around head and overlap as necessary before taping together. Excess can also be cut off if there is too much extra.

THINGS YOU'LL NEED...

- ❑ Paper bags, all sizes and colors (lunch sacks to grocery bags)
- ❑ Bibles
- ❑ Construction paper, all colors
- ❑ Glue or rubber cement
- ❑ Hole punch
- ❑ Magazines or newspapers
- ❑ Markers or crayons, all colors
- ❑ Pencils, pens
- ❑ Rulers
- ❑ Scissors
- ❑ Staplers, staples
- ❑ Straws
- ❑ Tape
- ❑ Unsharpened, new pencils
- ❑ Yarn
- ❑ Craft sticks, optional
- ❑ Sand, optional
- ❑ Candles, optional

MY OWN NOTES...
Use with lessons on...

134. Friendship Bracelet

Cut three strips, each 1 foot long and about 1 inch wide. (An easy way to make inch lengths is to trace a ruler since most of them are about an inch wide.) Fold strips in half for strength. Place the three ends together and staple together to hold.

Then, braid the strips (folding each strip as it fits into the braid) as shown. Staple ends together. Make a hole punch in both ends. Tie piece of yarn to each hole and use the yarn to tie the bracelet around a wrist.

Staple together at top

(These braided paper crafts can also be made with construction paper.)

135. Braided Belt

Cut six paper strips, each about 3 feet long and 1 inch wide. Make two strips each of any three colors.

Fold all strips in half longways. Braid one of each color together. Then braid the other set of colored strips. When both strips are braided, join together by taping or gluing and stapling together. Then, tape a piece of yarn (6" long) on each end. Use the yarn to tie the belt on.

136. Blessings Jump Rope

Cut six, nine, or more strips, each 3 feet long and 1 inch wide. Fold and braid the strips together until you have a good length for a jump rope. Put an extra staple or two in each end and where you add more lengths. Then tape over each junction point. This will make the jump rope stronger.

LUMINARIAS

137. Christmas Luminarias

Use any size paper bag as long as it has a stand-up bottom. Cut out shapes all over the bag—hearts, stars, J for Jesus, etc.

To set up a luminaria at home, put sand in bottom of bag. Then place a small candle (such as a votive or potpourri candle) in the center of the sand. Place outside to line a sidewalk or driveway or porch. *Caution:* Be sure to caution children to have parent help light the candle.

138. Easter Luminarias

Use any size bag with a stand-up bottom. Cut out strips of black paper and glue to bag, forming a stained glass window effect, coloring between shapes, or make the shape of a cross.

Black paper strips

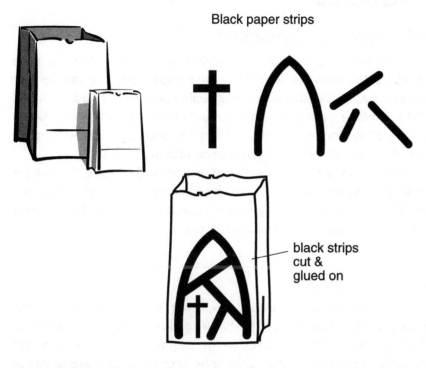

black strips cut & glued on

SCROLLS

139. Letter Scroll

Cut a strip of paper about 4" x 12" from a paper bag. Put glue on a straw, unsharpened pencil, or craft stick and wrap the paper around one at the top and bottom just enough to cover the straw, pencil or craft stick. Have students write a letter to someone on the scroll, roll it up, and tie with a length of yarn.

Idea: Have students write out Scripture verses and mail to each other like the early church did. Use with any lesson on the Apostle Paul's missionary journeys or early church lessons.

140. Bible Story Scrolls

Make a scroll from a 6" x 30" strip of paper bag. Draw one or more scenes from a Bible story. Tape or glue each end to a straw, unsharpened pencil, or craft stick.

Idea: Let students share their scroll-drawings with the class or have students mail these to friends, family members, or church shut-ins.

STUFFED BAGS

141. Paper Bag Characters

Students can use any of the materials you have available to make the characters from the day's lesson from paper bags. Use yarn for hair or beards. Make clothing out of construction paper. Each student should make something different, and then put all the characters together to make a Bible story scene. After making the characters, students lightly stuff the bags with magazine pages or newsprint and seal.

For a quick activity, use only paper bags and crayons. If you have time, let students add to the scene by making buildings, animals, trees, etc. These can be stuffed bags or even cut-outs from bags. Or, they may work on this project for several class times.

142. Solid Rock

Use small lunch-sized bags. Crumple bag lightly so it looks wrinkled. Students write on the front of the bag in marker: "I'm building my life on the Solid Rock." On the back of the bag, have students write out characteristics of a rock that apply to Jesus or things they are certain of because they believe in Jesus as Savior. Then stuff the bag with newsprint or magazine pages. Make it as solid as possible, leaving room to close bag. Close and tape or glue shut.

Use with lessons on living for Jesus or on Peter.

143. Good Graffiti Bricks

Write all over lunch bags in bright colors. Use sayings such as "God is great." "My God is awesome." "In times of need, call 1-800-God-helps." Stuff their bricks and tape or glue closed. Have students use to build a wall in the classroom.

144. Friendship Bag

Have students decide if they want their finished bag, which will be sealed, to be vertical or horizontal. Draw a line 1/2 to 1" inside the edges of the bag as a border in which to write. Write on the bag in colorful letters between the edge of the bag and the border: "I have good friends."

Then have each student pass his bag to every other classmate who signs it with encouraging, personalized messages such as: "Bill is praying for you." "Ann knows you can stand firm for Jesus." "Ted is glad you're part of our class." Students then stuff their bag and take home as a reminder that they are not alone in the struggles of daily life.

145. Fortress

Each student stuffs one or more bricks and writes his/her name on the side of each. Stack bricks in a corner of the room, building a castle type front. Hang a sign on it or over it that reads: "We are Christians banded together, and together we make a fortress against sin." Or, write: "Our God is a mighty Fortress, and we trust in Him."

146. God Made Me

Write Psalm 139:14a on the back of a large paper bag with brightly colored marker pens. Then, create a person that looks like the student on the front of bag—head, shirt, etc. Have each student trace his feet and cut out of another bag. Glue those to the bottom. Then have students trace their hands and draw arms. Cut those out and attach to the sides of the bag.

147. Animals

Lay a small, lunch-sized bag flat and color it the body color of any animal. Use construction paper and yarn for features or make one of the foam cup noses. Then, stuff the bags with newsprint or magazine pages and tape or glue closed.

Ideas: Make a paper bag nativity scene—Mary, Joseph, shepherds, small bag for Jesus in the manger, angels, donkeys, sheep. Depending on amount of time, students may each create one piece of the nativity and put all students' pieces together for a classroom nativity, or, they may make one or more pieces each week until they have a complete nativity to take home.

Can also be used with any Bible story that has animals in it such as Balaam's donkey, Creation, Noah's ark.

TORN PAPER

148. Old Rugged Cross

Have students cut out a cross of any size from paper bag. Tear small bits of paper bag and glue to the cross. Overlap some of the pieces, creating a rugged look. Add a yarn loop for hanging if desired.

Idea: Create a stuffed rock. Make three rugged crosses and glue to craft sticks. Stick bottom of craft stick into rock and glue or tape to make it stand up as an Easter scene at Calvary.

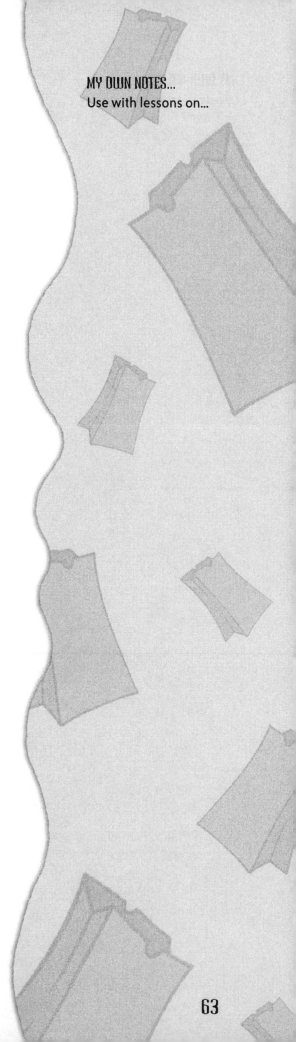

149. Cornucopia

A cone-shape of any size can be cut from a paper bag, as shown.

Shape does not have to be exact. Tear bits of paper and glue to cornucopia. Then, roll the shape as shown and glue or tape the edges.

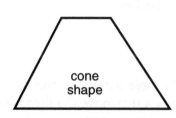
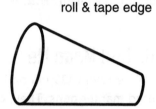

cone shape

roll & tape edge

Suggestion: Write blessings on bright cut-out shapes such as apples, oranges, grape-bunches, corn, pumpkins and place inside cornucopia. Or, cut out squares and circles, writing blessings on them.

BAG SCENES

150. Ark Scene

Use same concept as above. However, place the bag on its side and cut as shown.

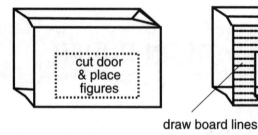

cut door
& place
figures

draw board lines

Leave a cut out for the door which students can raise when animals are inside. Draw board lines on the bag. Make Noah, his wife, their three sons and their wives as cylinder figures. Make two each of some of the animals and place inside the ark.

Idea: Use blue construction paper, cut waves in it, and place around the ark.

151. Nativity

Each student will need a large paper bag. Cut the bottom portion out of the lower front of bag, leaving at least 2" on each side. Cut "straw" from the cut out section of bag paper or from yellow construction paper. Spread this inside the bag. This will be the stable.

Make nativity characters from cylinders (a 6" high strip of construction paper, about 5" or 6" wide.) Draw the character on the strip first. Then roll paper into cylinder form and tape. Smaller cylinders can be used for animals. Place the characters inside bag for nativity scene.

152. God's Team Cap

Cut the front or back from a large paper bag. Lay it flat with any printing to the bottom. Trace a piece of 8-1/2" x 11" paper (or make an 8-1/2" x 11" rectangle using a ruler) and cut this rectangle out of the paper bag. Fold back one edge about 3 inches. This will be the front of the cap, and the folded piece will be the bill. Cut to round off bill edge as shown. Tape or glue.

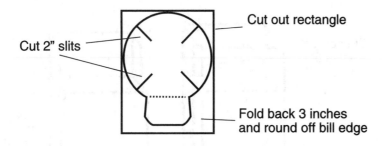

Cut 2" slits

Cut out rectangle

Fold back 3 inches and round off bill edge

Then round off the back edge. Make a 2" to 2-1/4" cut in each corner. Overlap cut edges and tape together as shown.

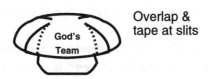

God's Team

Overlap & tape at slits

Decorate caps with markers or crayons.
Idea: Write on the front just above bill: "God's Team."

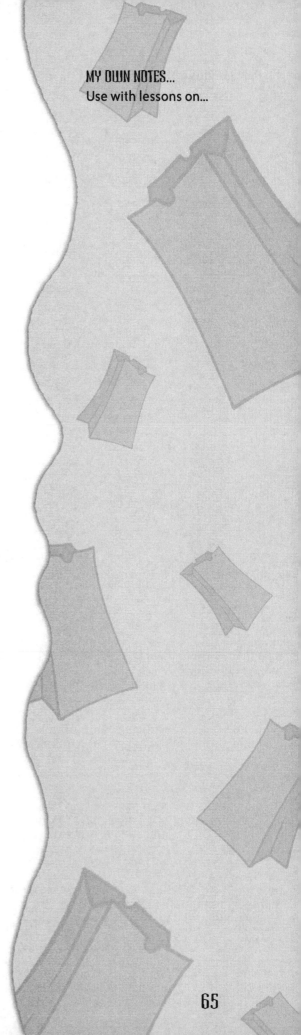

153. Suede Vest

Cut the bottom off a bag. Fold out flat and place as shown. Draw the shape shown with pencil, then cut.

Crumple the shape carefully so it doesn't tear. Crumple again and again until it looks wrinkled all over. Then, fold out flat again. (Vest may need to be turned inside-out to avoid having printing on outside of vest.) Tape the shoulder seams together after adding any coloring or writing desired.

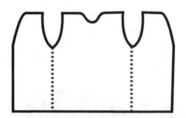 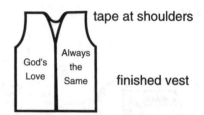

Idea: Write on the front with a dark color marker: "God's Love" on one side. Write: "Always the same" on the other. Decorate vest with markers as desired. If desired, remove paper from a crayon and rub the sides all over the vest.

154. Backpack

Use a large grocery bag for the backpack. Keep the side with printing (if any) toward the back. Cut down each corner about 5". Then fold the sides and front to inside of bag. This will leave a flap at the back.

Fold in the sides of the flap a little and tape.

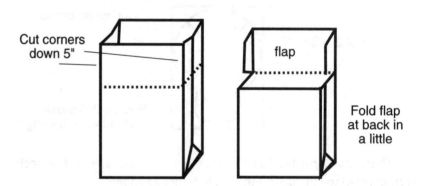

Punch a hole in each corner of the top edge of backpack. Add two holes at the bottom.

Cut a 20" piece of yarn. Thread through all holes, starting at one back corner. Tie at mid-back as drawstring to keep bag closed as well as a strap to hold. Braid three 25" lengths of yarn together to make a stronger strap. Thread through top and bottom holes as shoulder straps.

Idea: On front of backpack, students can write with markers or crayons: "I'm walkin' with my Lord." They may also decorate the entire backpack.

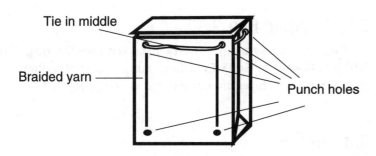

Tie in middle

Braided yarn

Punch holes

Can be used with lessons about Paul's missionary journey and the helpers who traveled with him. Or, with Abraham's journey from Ur to the land God gave him. Or, with lessons on the Wilderness wanderings of the Jews from Egypt to the Promised Land.

PENNANTS

155. Pennant

Cut a bag open and lay out flat. Fold in half. Cut the doubled paper into a triangular pennant shape, any size. It will make two pennants. Students may wish to draw the shape lightly in pencil first.

Suggestion: On one pennant, cut an oval at the broad end, leaving at least one inch as a solid band. Glue shapes together, leaving an opening beside the oval. Students can place their picture behind the oval and put their pennant up on their bedroom door or bulletin board.

Idea: Use markers to write "I Go For God" on the side. Decorate further if desired.

156. Praise Pennant

Cut one large pennant piece. Write in pencil "PRAISE GOD." Cover the letters in glue, then glitter.

ECOLOGY CRAFTS

157. Litter Bag

Decorate a grocery bag, as desired, with markers, crayons, stickers, or glitter. Write on bag: "Keep God's Earth Clean." Place the bag in the family car. Make a new litter bag as necessary.

Idea: Cut a scenic picture out of a magazine and glue on to the front of the bag. Cover with glue as a decoupage.

158. Recycle Bag

Decorate a bag as in Activity 157. Write on the bag: "Being a Faithful Steward of God's Creation." Put pictures of aluminum cans on the front or pictures of trees if paper is being recycled.

159. Poster

Cut open a bag and fold it out flat. Trim off the flaps that extend below the large rectangle. Use magazines to find pictures of nature, recycling efforts, or problem areas in your community. Have students write several ways to help solve the problem depicted. Display posters in the foyer or fellowship hall.

WINDSOCKS

160. Fish Windsock

Cut open a bag. Fold one side in half. From fold, cut a freehand fish shape, leaving the fold to connect the two sides. Cut out the mouth edge. Cut some scales and fins as shown and glue to fish.

Use a marker to draw eyes. Glue bottom edges together. To hang, punch two holes in mouth edge, and attach yarn.

Suggestion: On top of scales, write: "Keep our waters clean."

Idea: Use with Bible lessons on Peter and Andrew fishing, becoming fishers of men, Jonah, etc.

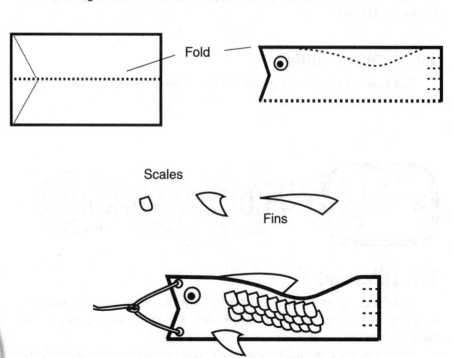

PAPER PLATE CRAFTS

ANGELS

8

161. Stand-up Angels

Cut a plate in quarters. Fold one quarter in half and cut across the bottom to make a flat edge. Fold two other quarters in half. Tape to first one as shown.

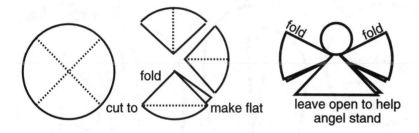

Add a line of glitter across top of wings. Fold out the bottom edge a little, until angel will stand.

162. Angel with Moveable Wings

Cut one plate in half. Place the two halves on a whole plate as shown with rounded edges downward.

Fasten at the X with paper fasteners. For head, trace around the top of a foam cup on a paper plate and cut out the circle. Glue to body. Spatter glue on the wings and sprinkle glitter on them.

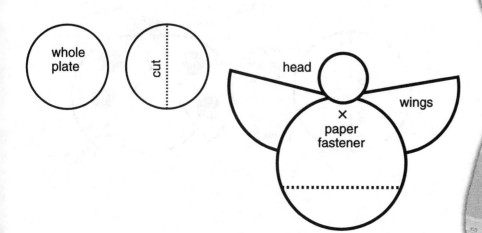

THINGS YOU'LL NEED...

- [ ] Paper plates
- [ ] Construction paper, all colors
- [ ] Craft sticks
- [ ] Glitter
- [ ] Glue or rubber cement
- [ ] Hole punch
- [ ] Magazines with scenic pictures
- [ ] Markers or crayons, all colors
- [ ] Paper fasteners
- [ ] Scissors
- [ ] Straws
- [ ] Foam cups
- [ ] Yarn

MY OWN NOTES...
Use with lessons on...

CRITTERS

163. Autograph Hound

Make a "hound" from a paper plate and construction paper. Cut two long floppy ears from any color of construction paper. Cut small circles for eyes and a triangle for nose and glue to plate as shown.

Draw a line for a mouth. Encourage students to have their friends autograph their hound.

Use to reinforce Bible truths such as God wants me to befriend others.

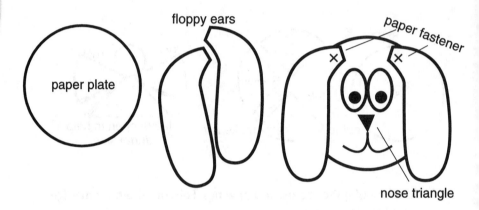

paper plate

floppy ears

paper fastener

nose triangle

164. Bug

Color two plates red. Cut one plate in half. Place the two halves on a whole plate as shown.

Fasten at X with paper fasteners. Cut a small circle of black construction paper for head and glue on. Cut several black circles for spots on bug and glue them on, or draw them with a marker.

Use with lessons on Creation, Noah's ark, God's creatures, etc.

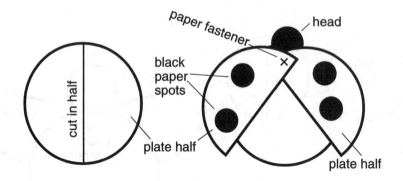

paper fastener

head

black paper spots

cut in half

plate half

plate half

165. Turkey Blessings

Cut a plate in half. Then cut several bright feathers (ovals about 1" to 2" wide and 3" to 4" long with short slits along the edges.). Write one of God's blessing on each feather: friends, family, home, God's love, the Bible, my friends, etc.

 feather

 wattle

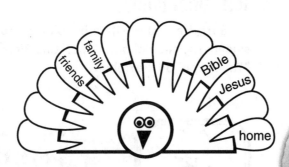

Color plate brown. For head, cut a circle out of light brown or yellow construction paper. (Trace the bottom of a foam cup and cut out.) Glue to center of plate-half. Draw eyes and glue on a small triangle of brown paper for beak. Cut 2-inch teardrop shape from red paper and glue to bottom of head under beak for wattle. Glue feathers to plate-half.

Use with lessons on thanksgiving or at the holiday.

166. Big-Feet Critters

Students trace their own feet on construction paper or paper bag and cut out. Have them draw their face on a plate and add construction paper hair. For a body, they can make a stuffed paper bag. Glue or tape face and feet to bag.

RIBBONS AND AWARDS

167. Best Dad

Color a plate blue or yellow. Write "#1 DAD" or "BEST DAD" in big, colorful letters. Cut two ribbons from blue construction paper. Ribbons should be 1" to 2" wide and 4" to 6" long. Tape or glue onto bottom edge of plate.

Idea: Give Dad a big blue ribbon for Father's Day or surprise him with one after a lesson on honoring parents. Write on ribbon: "I love you."

(See also under Weavings.)

168. Best Mom

Make a ribbon as above. Write "#1 MOM" or "Best Mom in the World" on plate. On ribbon, write: "I love you."

169. Best Pastor

Surprise Pastor with a big blue ribbon from the class. Have each student sign the ribbons. Write: "God Bless Our Pastor" on the plate and "Thank You" on the ribbons.

FLOWERS

170. Bloom

Use plate as flower. Write on inside of plate: "Bloom for God." Color several different colors on rim. Cut a long green stem with leaves from construction paper and staple to plate. Write on stem or leaves ways to bloom for God (pray, learn, worship, obey).

Idea: Use the smaller dessert paper plates, color several and make the stems for each. Write ways to bloom for God in the center of each plate and put a bouquet of flowers together.

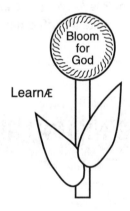

Color different colors on rim

Option: Create a garden in the classroom by crumpling up green construction paper for grass and planting the flowers in it. Tape stems to craft sticks. Tape craft sticks to floor. Spread crumpled green paper around them. Build a white fence from construction paper and craft sticks. Place around the green grass and flowers.

171. Sunflowers

Color a plate yellow. Add lots of brown dots in the middle with marker.

Option: On stem, write: "Jesus is my Sonshine."

MARIONETTES

172. Whatchamacallit Critter

Use a straw for a handle. Tie five lengths of yarn (about 10" to 12" each) around the straw. (Glue if necessary to make them stay.)

Punch four holes in plate for legs and one for neck. See illustration.

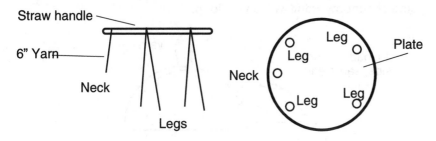

Tie yarn from handle to holes in plate.

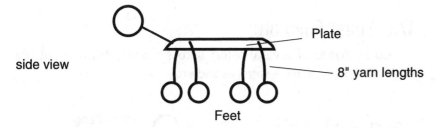

Then, cut four feet, any size and shape, and attach to plate with 8" yarn lengths. (Students may want to weave several strands of yarn together to make bigger legs.) Make a head for the critter from another plate. Use imagination.

Then, attach the head to the handle and to front of plate with the 6" length. Color critter as desired. Manipulate the critter with the handle.

Option: Write on the back of the plate: "God sees the beauty in everyone."

173. Character Marionette

Make a marionette as above, except keep plate upright as shown.

Attach only the head and hands of your character/critter to the handle.

Idea: Make characters from a Bible story and use them to re-tell it, or just make a "you" puppet.

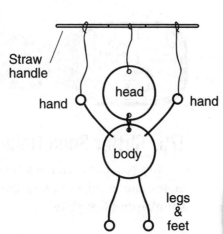

RAINBOWS

174. Promise Rainbow

Cut a paper plate in half. Color outside of both halves in rainbow colors (Top to bottom colors are: red, orange, yellow, green, blue, indigo, violet). Staple together. Cut two cloud shapes from white paper. Write on both: "God keeps His promises." Glue one to each side of rainbow. Hang with a yarn loop.

1 cloud on each side, same end   yarn

175. Spiral Rainbow

Color stripes of several colors across a plate. Begin at outside edge and cut plate into a spiral as shown.

cut in a spiral   yarn to hang

Attach a yarn loop.
Suggestion: Hang by a window and watch it spin in the breeze.

SNOWFLAKES

176. Glitter Snowflakes

Use scissors to create a snowflake from a plate. Cut shapes from edges and middle of plate. Spread glue around the snowflake and sprinkle on silver glitter.

Option: Snowflake Mobile—Have students make several and hang a new one every Sunday they come to class as an attendance registry. Can be hung as part of a student's personal mobile in the classroom to take home at the end of a quarter or put them all together in one big classroom mobile.

Idea: Announce a "blizzard" contest and see how many snowflakes students can accumulate during a quarter by adding one each Sunday they come to the classroom mobile.

Option: Make the above snowflake and cut some smaller snowflakes from another plate. Attach to large snowflake with yarn or string.

 WREATHS

177. Christmas Wreath

Cut center from paper plate. Color the wreath shape green or red. Cut a 2" x 5" piece from red or green construction paper. Round off at top and bottom to look like a candle. Add a yellow or orange flame to candle with glue. Glue candle to center bottom of wreath. Add a red yarn loop to hang.

Option: Roll 2 to 3 pieces of green construction paper and crumple lightly in accordion fashion. Glue to rim of paper plate. Add candle.

178. Wreath Scenes

Cut center from one paper plate to form a wreath shape. On a whole plate, glue scene from a magazine page such as winter scene, waterfall, boating picture, etc. (Picture should be no larger than the hole in wreath shape.) After gluing the scene on inside of whole plate, staple, glue, or tape the wreath shape over it. Glitter may be added to outside of wreath shape. Add yarn to hang.

 PLEDGE PLAQUES

179. Christian Flag

Write Pledge of Allegiance to this flag on the plate. Cut out some blue and red crosses and glue around edge of plate.

Pledge to the Christian flag

I pledge allegiance to the Christian flag and to the Savior for whose kingdom it stands. One Savior, crucified, risen, and coming again with life and liberty for all who believe.

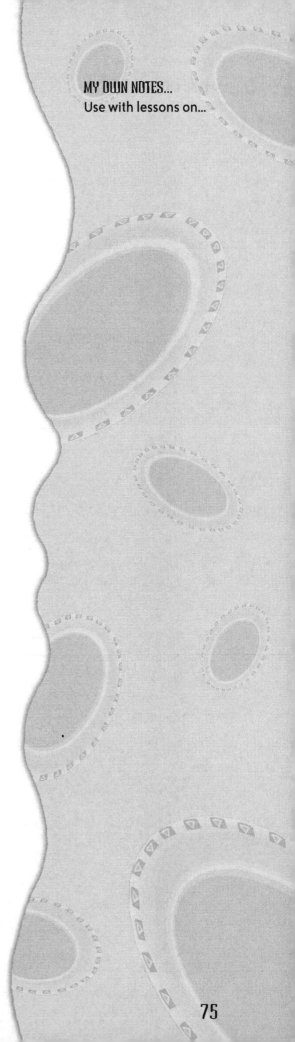

180. Flag Pledge

Write the pledge of allegiance or the national anthem on a plate. Then, draw some small flags around the pledge.

Option: Mount the plate in the middle of a sunburst. Make two large fan-folded angel wing starburst ornaments (chapter 5). Tape long edges together. Basic directions for a sunburst are in Chapter 5, Craft #107.

Option: Tape streamers of paper decorated with glitter to the back of the sunburst so that they extend below it. Streamers should be in proportion to the size of the sunburst, but approximately 2" to 3" wide by 18" to 24" long.

181. Bible

Write Pledge of Allegiance to the Bible in center of plate. Add Bible stickers if you have them on hand or draw Bibles around the rim.

Pledge to the Bible

I pledge allegiance to the Bible, God's holy Word, a lamp unto my feet and a light unto my path. Its words will I hide in my heart that I might not sin against God.

182. Pledge Wall Hanging

Students make the three plaques above. Then, use red or blue yarn to connect them and hang together.

WEAVING

183. Best Dad

Color a plate any color. Write "Best Dad" or "#1 DAD" lightly in pencil. Using a hole punch, punch out holes along the letters at least 1/4" apart. Weave yarn through holes either across (like shoelaces) or vertically to outline the letters. Cut two ribbons from blue construction paper. Ribbons should be 1" to 2" wide and 4" to 6" long. Tape or glue onto bottom edge of plate.

Idea: Give to Dad for Father's Day or surprise him with one after a lesson on honoring parents. Write on ribbon: "I love you."

184. Best Mom

Write "#1 MOM" or "Best Mom in the World" on plate. Make plate weaving as above. On ribbon, write: "I love you."

185. Woven Cross

Draw cross shape on paper plate. Cut four slits in plate on vertical edges. Leave at least 1/4" between end of cut and the crossbar. Then make four slits on horizontal crossbar, leaving at least 1/4" between end of cut and vertical bar. Then, cut a 30" length of yarn and wrap through, up, and down slits as shown.

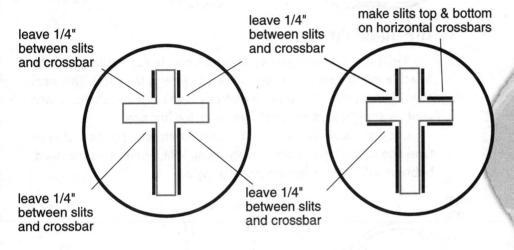

leave 1/4" between slits and crossbar

leave 1/4" between slits and crossbar

make slits top & bottom on horizontal crossbars

leave 1/4" between slits and crossbar

leave 1/4" between slits and crossbar

For crossbar, students can choose whether to use same or different color of yarn. While wrapping through the slits, also weave through some of the up and down yarns. Tape ends to back of plate.

weave yarn in and out through slits

186. Best Pastor Gift

Surprise Pastor with a big blue ribbon from the class. Have each student sign the ribbons. Write: "World's Best Pastor" on the ribbons.

77

CHENILLE STEM CRAFTS

WEARABLES

THINGS

YOU'LL NEED...

- ❏ Chenille stems
- ❏ Construction paper, all colors
- ❏ Craft sticks
- ❏ Glue or rubber cement
- ❏ Markers or crayons, all colors
- ❏ Paint, tempera or acrylic
- ❏ Foam cups
- ❏ Yarn
- ❏ Magnets, small pieces, optional

MY OWN NOTES...

Use with lessons on...

187. Head Bobbers

Twist two stems together at both ends to form a large circle. Attach another stem by twisting one end tightly to the circle. This stem should stand straight up at 90 degrees to the original circle. Attach another straight stem about 5" away from the first one.

Cut two hearts (about 3" x 3") from construction paper. Glue or tape one to the top of each straight stem. When placed on the head, bobbers will "bob" around but stay upright.

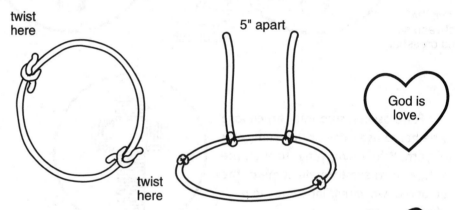

twist here

5" apart

twist here

God is love.

Option: Write God is Love on each heart.

Alternative: Trace the top of a foam cup onto white paper and cut this circle out. Cut circle in half. Color rainbow stripes on each half-circle. Glue or tape one rainbow to each of the two upright stems.

Alternative: Any shape can be attached to the ends of the upright, straight stems.

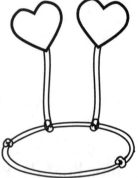

188. Heart Chain

Bend a chenille stem in half. With the point facing downward, bend the two sides into a heart shape. Twist ends together. Make several hearts, linking together before twisting ends together. Link together enough hearts to make a necklace, belt, or garland.

Option: Make a hanger for mobile by tying two chenille stems together in an X. Tie at the middle with yarn and leave a loop of yarn for hanging. Hang several hearts from a mobile.

Reinforce themes of love, friendship, encouraging others, Greatest Commandment.

189. Spiral Wearables

Make several spirals of different colors by twisting stems around a pencil. Slip spirals over a piece of yarn to make necklaces, bracelets, or belts.

190. Friendship Twists

Twist three different colors of stems together from top to bottom. Then form a circle and twist ends together. Can also twist around a piece of yarn and tie ends together.

Suggestion: Twist together red, orange, yellow stems. Use to remind students of Three Friends in Fiery Furnace. Then, twist a white stem all the way around the others to remind students that Jesus was also there.

Option: Cut the finished twist into three sections and twist ends together to make three friendship rings.

ANIMALS AND PEOPLE

191. Fish

Form a simple fish with one chenille stem as shown. Twist stem together where it crosses at end of body, leaving about 2" of each end for the tail fin.

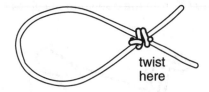

twist
here

Use with lessons such as: Jonah, Fishers of Men, Feeding 5000.

192. Window Butterfly

Form one chenille stem in a C-shape and another into a backward C. Twist the ends of each around a craft stick to form butterfly wings. Cut two 2" lengths from a chenille stem and glue to one end of the craft stick for feelers. Cut a 10" length of yarn and tie one end to the top end of one butterfly wing. Hang butterfly in a window.

Option: Glue a small bit of magnet to back of craft stick.

193. Flowers

Cut three stems in half. Bend each of the six lengths into a petal shape and twist the ends together. Bend the twisted ends down about 1/2". Hold all six petals together by the 1/2" ends. Wrap the end of a green stem around the six petal ends and twist tightly together. Bend the green stem down to make flower stem. Cut a green chenille stem in half and bend each piece into a leaf shape. Twist ends together, then twist ends of leaves around the flower stem.

194. Turkey

Turn a foam cup on its side. Form a large teardrop shape with a yellow chenille stem and twist the ends together. Poke the twisted end into the end of cup bottom as shown.

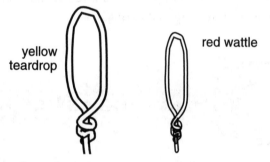

yellow teardrop

red wattle

Bend the top of teardrop shape forward a little to look like turkey's head. Cut a red stem in half. Bend one length into a teardrop shape and twist the ends together. Poke the end into the bottom of cup just below head to make a wattle.

Bend 6 different colors of stems in half. Form a teardrop shape with each and twist ends together. Poke the ends of teardrop shapes into cup about 1/2" apart and 1/2" from the open end of cup as shown.

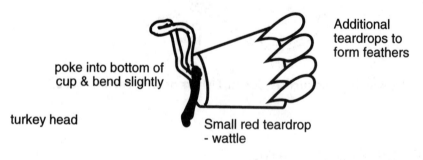

poke into bottom of cup & bend slightly

Additional teardrops to form feathers

turkey head

Small red teardrop - wattle

195. People

Trace the bottom of a foam cup to make a circle and cut out. Turn cup upside-down; draw a face on the circle. Glue circle to side of cup at bottom edge. Cut a chenille stem in half. Poke one end of each half-stem into opposite sides of cup for arms. Bend the exposed ends of stems a little to look like hands. Color front of cup for character's clothes. Add construction paper hats or clothing.

196. Mouse

Color a cup gray and turn on its side. Color the bottom end gray also. Draw two eyes on the end of cup. Cut a gray chenille stem into thirds. Bend two of the pieces into teardrop shapes and twist ends together for ears. Poke ears into cup at top edge above eyes. Cut two gray or pink stems into fourths. Poke four of the small pieces into each side of the cup at the bottom of the face for whiskers. Tape a whole gray or pink stem to the bottom of the open end of cup for a tail. Curl tail slightly around a pencil if desired.

Option: Make other animals using mouse directions. Change ears and tail slightly to correspond with different animals such as dog, cat, pig, donkey, cow.

197. Springy Characters

Twist a stem around and around a pencil to form a spiral. Straighten out both ends of the spiral about 1/2". Poke one end into the bottom of an upside-down foam cup.

Cut two circles from construction paper. On the other end of spiral, glue the two circles with the 1/2" of stem between. Draw a face on one circle. Glue small pieces of yarn on it for hair. Take another chenille stem and twist around first stem for arms.

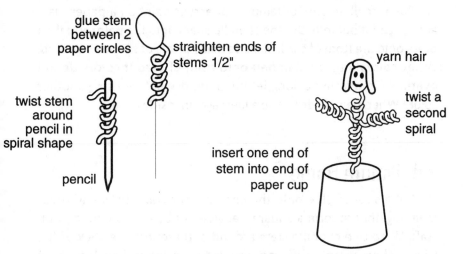

glue stem between 2 paper circles

straighten ends of stems 1/2"

yarn hair

twist stem around pencil in spiral shape

pencil

twist a second spiral

insert one end of stem into end of paper cup

Suggestion: Make several springy characters and stick them into the bottom of an upside-down paper plate. Color on the plate to make a scene, such as grass, water, etc. Make a favorite Bible story scene.

198. Hope Caterpillars

Twist a green stem around a pencil to make a spiral. Slip spiral off pencil. Bend out one coil at one end of the spiral. Stick a large circle of construction paper to the coil and draw on a face.

Option: Glue a small bit of magnet to the back of spiral. Place caterpillar on refrigerator.

CARDS/GIFTS

199. Texture Cards

Fold a piece of construction paper in half to make a card. On front of card draw a large shape such as a heart, flower, or Christmas tree. Outline the shape with brightly colored markers. Write a message inside card.

Cut several chenille stems into thirds. Curl each small piece around a pencil. Do not twist closed. Glue the curls flat onto the front of card, filling in the shape drawn. Let dry and encourage students to give the card to someone.

200. Stamped Card

Fold a piece of construction paper in half to make a card. Bend a chenille stem into a shape (circle, heart, triangle, square), leaving about half of the stem straight for a handle. Bend the shape so that it can stand flat on a table and the handle will stick straight up in the air.

Put a small amount of tempera or acrylic paint on a paper plate and spread it out thin. Dip the chenille shape into the paint and then press onto the front of card. Make as many prints of shape as desired. Other colors may be stamped onto front of card if colors do not overlap. (To overlap colors, let the paint dry before using another color.) When paint is dry, write a message on inside of card.

201. Picture Frame

Put a spot of glue onto the ends of four craft sticks and press them together to form a square. Let glue dry before continuing with craft. Wrap one chenille stem around and around one stick of the frame. Then, wrap a different colored stem around each of the 3 remaining sticks.

Option: Wrap stems closely around the frame sticks, using several for each side of the frame. (This will cover entire frame, allowing none of the sticks to show through.) Glue a picture to back of frame, so it shows through to the front.

202. Pencil Holder or Candy Cup

Use 1 foam cup and at least 10 chenille stems for this craft. Cut the stems in half. Poke end of one stem into the bottom of cup and then wrap stem toward top of cup. Bend other end over top of cup. Continue with the stems until cup is covered.

Suggestion: Put some pencils or wrapped candies in the cup and give as a gift.

VERSE CRAFTS

203. Jacob's Ladder

Use two stems for sides of the ladder. Cut two other stems into thirds. Cut several straws into 2" or 3" lengths. Put 1/3 length of stem through a straw piece and then wrap one end around each side of the ladder to form a rung. Add five more rungs.

Cut a 1" x 3" strip of construction paper. Write on the paper: "I am with you," or "God watches over me" (Gen. 28:10-17). Attach to ladder rung.

204. Balloons

Turn a foam cup upside down. Decorate cup with crayons or pictures from magazines. Write in marker: "Jesus lifts me up." Cut four or five balloon shapes (ovals) from brightly colored construction paper. Glue or tape each balloon to a half chenille stem. Poke ends of stems into cup bottom.

205. Words

Form letters from chenille stems to spell easy words such as: "Jesus," "Love," or "Bible." Form one letter from each chenille stem. For letters that are not closed (J, L, V, etc.), form a small loop at the top end to attach to yarn for hanging.

Cut a length of yarn for each letter. Tie each length of yarn to the hanger and one letter.

Option: Make a hanger for mobile by tying two chenille stems together in an X. Tie at the middle with yarn and leave a loop of yarn for hanging. Hang letters from mobile.

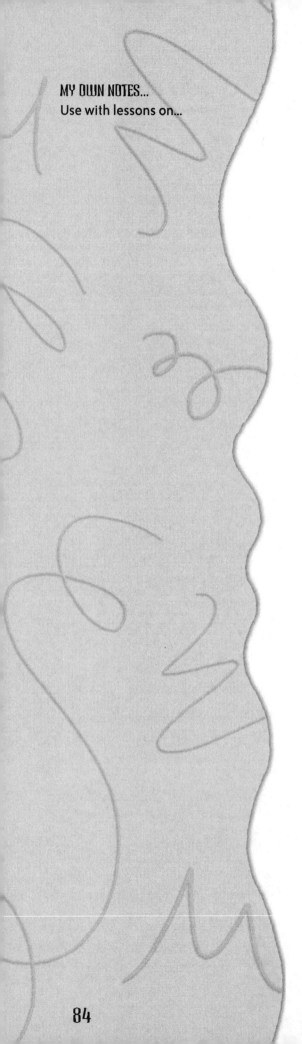

ORNAMENTS

206. Candy Cane Ornament

Twist a red and white stem together from top to bottom. Then twist top to form a cane.

Alternatives: Twist a green and a red stem together from top to bottom. Then, form a circle for a wreath. Glue on a red bow made from a 6" length of yarn.

Bend a green stem into the shape of a Christmas tree. Twist the ends together.

QUICK CRAFTING SUGGESTIONS AND HELPS

INSTANT CRAFT HELPS

Use these helpful suggestions when looking for something different to do. Some will have to be prepared by you or another volunteer beforehand.

Shrink~Crafts

Foam meat trays or foam plates can be used to make shrink-crafts. Cut a pattern from paper. (A good size is larger than 2" and smaller that 6".) Reproducible coloring pictures can be cut out and traced for patterns. Or, use circles, hearts, squares, etc. and color a picture or write a verse. Crayons and permanent markers will work equally well.

Cut out the item and color it. Place several items on a cookie sheet and bake at 350 degrees for about 3 minutes. If curling occurs when baking, flatten with a spatula when still warm. Poke a hole for hanging either before or after baking.

Instant Light Switch Covers

Index cards are the perfect size for light switch covers. Decorate as desired on the unlined side and cut the hole using a real light switch cover as a sample. Clear light switch plates can be used to mount the students' creations behind.

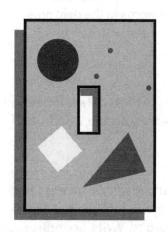

THINGS YOU'LL NEED...

- ❑ Colored chalk
- ❑ Craft sticks
- ❑ Glue or rubber cement
- ❑ Index cards
- ❑ Markers or crayons, all colors
- ❑ Paints or ink
- ❑ Reproducible coloring pictures
- ❑ Foam meat trays
- ❑ Foam plates
- ❑ Unsharpened, new pencils

MY OWN NOTES...
Use with lessons on...

QUICK IDEAS FOR EMERGENCIES

Use the following no-preparation/no-help crafts for times when there is no time to plan ahead.

Stamps for Ink or Paints

Foam meat trays make wonderfully simple stamps. Cut a square or circle from meat tray. Draw a design or shape lightly with pencil. Then use the end of an unsharpened pencil to make a groove in all edges of design or shape.

Spread a thin layer of paint or ink in a paper plate. (Ink pad can be used if shape is smaller than size of ink pad.) Dip the stamp into ink or paint, then press onto piece of paper to make print. Foam stamps can be washed and reused.

Banners/Murals/Posters/Collages

Set out the newsprint/freezer wrap or large sheets of construction paper and any of the following items: Crayons, markers, colored chalk, magazine pages, scissors, glue. Tell students to make a banner (mural, poster, collage) on families, Bible lesson theme, etc.

Footprints

Have students make footprints from any type of paper and use as a follow the leader path or a memory verse path or make a personal poster about ways to follow Jesus.

Make a memory verse path by writing one word or phrase of the memory verse on one of a set of footprints. Place around the room and have students follow the words in the right order.

This idea can also be used with handprints.

Hearts

Cut out various sizes of hearts. Make a class mural on Loving Others or create a picture of animals, people, clouds, etc. from the hearts.

Mobiles

See index for specific ideas. Or, give students each a paper plate. Punch holes around edge of plate and attach yarn of varying lengths from which to hang shapes. Write Scriptures, praise statements, or prayer thoughts on the shapes, punch hole and tie onto mobile with yarn.

Paper Plate Masks

Give each student a paper plate. Put out scissors, glue, glitter, construction paper, yarn, etc. Tell students to make an animal or Bible character. Punch a hole in each side. Use yarn to tie mask on.

Option: Have students create heads of people or animals from paper plates to use as puppets. Then, attach a craft stick to bottom, back edge of plate to hold up as a puppet.

Paper Bag Puppets

Give each student a lunch sized bag. Turn it upside down. Use crayons or markers to create a character from the day's Bible lesson.

Bible Costumes

Give students one or more large paper bags. Each will create a Bible costume, such as soldier uniform, priestly robe, king's clothing, etc.

Just for Fun

Have a Spur-of-the-Moment silly hat contest. Give each student one or two paper plates. They may use any items from your craft closet that you choose.

Suggestion: Have class model their creations for another class, or have that class judge the hats. Prize can be a quickly-made blue ribbon from a paper plate and construction paper, or a promise coupon for a treat at the next class meeting.

Craft Stick Fun

Give students some craft sticks and glue. They may also use markers or whatever else you choose to set out for them. Have them make a fortress, build a town or castle, create a railroad tracks and train cars, or whatever they choose.

ALPHABETICAL INDEX OF CRAFTS

The number given is the craft number rather than the page number.
Crafts are numbered consecutively through the book.

BIBLE TRUTHS AND STORIES INDEX

The number given is the craft number rather than the page number.
Crafts are numbered consecutively through the book.

GENERAL INDEX

The number given is the craft number rather than the page number.
Crafts are numbered consecutively through the book.

CHAPTER INDEX

The number given is the craft number rather than the page number.
Crafts are numbered consecutively through the book.

The Word at Work . . .
Around the World

What would you do if you wanted to share God's love with children on the streets of your city? That's the dilemma David C. Cook faced in 1870s Chicago. His answer was to create literature that would capture children's hearts.

Out of those humble beginnings grew a worldwide ministry that has used literature to proclaim God's love and disciple generation after generation. Cook Communications Ministries is committed to personal discipleship—to helping people of all ages learn God's Word, embrace his salvation, walk in his ways, and minister in his name.

Opportunities—and Crisis

We live in a land of plenty—including plenty of Christian literature! But what about the rest of the world? Jesus commanded, "Go and make disciples of all nations" (Matt. 28:19) and we want to obey this commandment. But how does a publishing organization "go" into all the world?

There are five times as many Christians around the world as there are in North America. Christian workers in many of these countries have no more than a New Testament, or perhaps a single shared copy of the Bible, from which to learn and teach.

We are committed to sharing what God has given us with such Christians.

A vital part of Cook Communications Ministries is our international outreach, Cook Communications Ministries International (CCMI). Your purchase of this book, and of other books and Christian-growth products from Cook, enables CCMI to provide Bibles and Christian literature to people in more than 150 languages in 65 countries.

Cook Communications Ministries is a not-for-profit, self-supporting organization. Revenues from sales of our books, Bible curriculum, and other church and home products not only fund our U.S. ministry, but also fund our CCMI ministry around the world. One hundred percent of donations to CCMI go to our international literature programs.

CCMI reaches out internationally in three ways:

· Our premier International Christian Publishing Institute (ICPI) trains leaders from nationally led publishing houses around the world to develop evangelism and discipleship materials to transform lives in their countries.

· We provide literature for pastors, evangelists, and Christian workers in their national language. We provide study helps for pastors and lay leaders in many parts of the world, such as China, India, Cuba, Iran, and Vietnam.

· We reach people at risk—refugees, AIDS victims, street children, and famine victims—with God's Word. CCMI puts literature that shares the Good News into the hands of people at spiritual risk—people who might die before they hear the name of Jesus and are transformed by his love.

Word Power—God's Power

Faith Kidz, RiverOak, Honor, Life Journey, Victor, NexGen — every time you purchase a book produced by Cook Communications Ministries, you not only meet a vital personal need in your life or in the life of someone you love, but you're also a part of ministering to José in Colombia, Humberto in Chile, Gousa in India, or Lidiane in Brazil. You help make it possible for a pastor in China, a child in Peru, or a mother in West Africa to enjoy a life-changing book. And because you helped, children and adults around the world are learning God's Word and walking in his ways.

Thank you for your partnership in helping to disciple the world. May God bless you with the power of his Word in your life.

For more information about our international ministries, visit www.ccmi.org.